Just Kidding

Surviving the Chaos of Family Life

Gail S. Hettrick

DORRANCE
PUBLISHING CO
EST. 1920
PITTSBURGH, PENNSYLVANIA 15238

Dorrance Publishing Co
585 Alpha Drive
Pittsburgh, PA 15238
Visit our website at *www.dorrancebookstore.com*

ISBN: 978-1-6386-7016-2
EISBN: 978-1-6386-7965-3

Just Kidding

Surviving the Chaos of Family Life

Dedicated to my four sons, Robert, Phillip, Andrew and David. You are my greatest joys!

Thank you to *The Vindicator* for permission to reprint these columns. I will always be grateful to *The Vindicator* for hiring me as a columnist. It was a job that I couldn't believe I got paid to do.

Some of these writings appeared in a regional business newspaper.

Special Thanks to Jeff Schoch, copy editor extraordinaire. Without your expertise and attention to detail, I would have had many sleepless nights making final edits to this manuscript.

Also special thanks to my neighbor and photographic genius, Tina Cutright. Reflections of Time Photography did an amazing job on the front cover photo and author photo.

Contents

Foreword

But Seriously —

For years, I would be talking with a family member or friend and they would stop abruptly and say, "This isn't going to end up in the paper, is it?"

It often did.

Writing a twice-weekly column, I was always looking for subjects. I was commissioned by the *The Vindicator* to write about unsung heroes and everyday people doing remarkable things. I absolutely LOVED writing those stories! Those could fill a book. Getting consent from the subjects a decade and a half later makes doing that impossible.

Every once in a while, I would write about something that happened in my family. After my first year at *The Vindicator*, the editor suggested I write one column a week about heroes and the other column about family. People were enjoying the stories. I never loved a job more!

It was truly my children who endured the brunt of my writing. For the most part, they handled it well. A few were too young to remember NOT being in print! Every once in a while, I would strike a nerve with a child and if caught soon enough, the story would not be submitted. Occasionally, something I thought was just a silly, funny story would run and a child would be upset. We would work through it. All would survive. The hazards of living with someone who may tell the world about anything you do!

While I always wanted to write a book, I never considered compiling my columns into a book until I decided to digitize them. Pulling the columns out of storage, I realized the newsprint was fading. In time, all the stories would be lost forever.

As I started digitizing, I found myself laughing out loud. I had completely forgotten some of the events. The kids, now adults, started reading them from a whole new perspective — and enjoying it immensely!

I realized I needed to not only digitize the columns but compile a collection of them for my children to remember forever.

To EVERYONE who is found in the pages of this book, I'm so grateful and blessed to have you in my life. THANK YOU for your kindness and understanding as I "used" your words in my writing. You too, are now immortalized forever in these pages.

To my children — Robert, Phillip, Andrew and David—you have blessed my life more than you will ever know. The laughter, the tears, the growing through the years. Being your mom is the greatest joy of my life. I hope when you have families, you will enjoy them as much as I enjoyed raising you. Forever Your Mom.

Gail

What Did I Do Before I Had Kids?

Hobbies and Interests, the job application read. Finally, a fun question, I thought. After having regurgitated my life's work history and schooling, this would be a breeze.

Ten minutes later, the line is blank.

MY hobbies… MY interests…

Most of my adult life has been spent having children and raising them. Do chauffeuring, spectating and boo-boo kissing count as hobbies?

I used to have hobbies. I can't exactly remember them right now but I know I was always busy doing something.

Parenthood has a way of causing memory loss.

It is almost as if, with every spit-up and diaper change, a few brain cells die, until somewhere between the second and third child, a stupor sets in and even completing a simple sentence becomes impossible.

Memory is not all that is lost in parenthood. I don't believe there is any way to prepare for the loss of self that happens when you have children.

It starts with the birth of the first. As you hold that babe in your arms the world becomes smaller and suddenly, you are focused solely on this small life. You will do anything for this child.

As siblings arrive, the feelings intensify — along with the chaos. Your entire world revolves around bedtimes, naptimes and feeding times. All intermixed with moments of insanity.

My husband and I wanted a large family. With the birth of our fourth son, we decided that was large enough.

Now, with Robert, 12; Phillip, 9; and Andrew, 7, all in school, the days are quiet for 2 year-old David and me at home — until 3 o'clock rolls around. I have found that if I am not at a sporting event or a school function, I am driving to one.

Sometimes, as I sit behind the wheel, heading into town for the fifth time that afternoon, with one child crying and two arguing in the back of the van, I ponder what I would be doing right now had I chosen a different path.

Scuba diving in Aruba? Skiing in Vail? Cruising the Caribbean? Perhaps.

But that would have meant no first steps, no big hugs and sticky kisses, no middle-of-the-night cries for Mommy, no wilted flower bouquets.

My life will be complete without worldly travels and exotic excursions. But it would not have been complete or fulfilling without my children.

There is an entire spectrum of emotions that goes untapped until one becomes a parent.

My children have given me my greatest joys and my deepest sorrows. They have brought out the very best in me, causing me to reach deep within myself to achieve at this "Mom" role.

They also have brought out the very worst in me, at times stirring up an inner monster of sorts.

As much as I strive to give them the very best of me, I have received so much more from them. They have forced me, despite myself, to be a better person.

Hobbies and Interests. Maybe I'll leave that one blank for right now.

I know I can answer the next question: "What has given you your greatest sense of accomplishment?"

Now that one is truly easy; Child 1, 2, 3 and 4.

Home Movie Memories — Some I'd Like to Forget

We were spending a family evening watching home movies.

I just love home movies — watching the children running around in their toddler waddle, listening to their little voices, laughing at their funny antics. It's all wonderful family entertainment.

What I learned this particular evening, however, is that some scenes in life are better left unrecorded.

The evening began innocently enough. We had delved into our video archives and found a videotape of Andrew's first steps.

Andrew is our third child. At the time of the taping, Robert was 5, Phillip was 2-1/2.

It was such a happy scene, videotaped in our living room. Daddy was holding Andrew, while Robert and Phillip, the encouraging older brothers, were happily bouncing around in the background, excited to see their little brother's first steps.

The video begins as Dad scoots across the floor, holding out his hands.

"Come on, Andrew, walk to Daddy," he beckons the toddler.

Andrew's mouth is open, his two little teeth shining through the dribble running down his chin.

He takes a precarious step, then another. As he falls into Daddy's arms, his cheering section erupts.

Robert pats Andrew on the head, "You did so good!" he encourages his little brother.

"Sooo dood!" echoes Phillip.

The tape continues, with Robert and Phillip taking turns catching the unsteady new walker.

When one is not catching, he can be seen in the background

jumping up and down with great excitement over this wonderful event.

The conclusion of "Andrew's First Steps" shows the three boys on Daddy's belly, all covered in happy toddler slobber.

It was beautiful. A moment in time, caught on tape for our family to remember forever.

It was so sweet and endearing, it brought a tear to my eye.

When we put in the next tape, I broke out into a full-blown bawl.

Someone had the bright idea to flash forward five years and watch David's first steps on tape.

It sounded innocent enough for me.

Unfortunately, innocence had left our household years before.

When David began his journey into the walking masses, he too was one year old. His brothers were 11, 7, and 5.

Times had changed.

The tape begins with a happy mother.

"Do you want to walk today?" I cooed to the excited toddler.

"Robert, lean him up against the corner of the couch." Then changing into my baby voice, "So da big boy can walk to Mommy!"

The camera reveals an 11-year-old tugging at what appears to be a dressed, wet noodle.

They fall to the ground. They wrestle. The two brother sidekicks join in.

The camera goes black.

Next scene. The tape is rolling again, and David is situated beside the couch.

A sweet Mom's voice, "Come here, David. Walk to Mommy."

He falls. As Robert attempts to pick him up, David becomes a wet noodle again.

The sidekicks try to help. Once again, a wrestling match breaks out.

Mom's sweet voice is becoming impatient. Her words are cut off as she shuts off the camera again.

The picture returns to find a determined, yet somewhat confused toddler preparing to take a few steps.

He moves a foot.

Andrew dives in front of the lens. "Don't jump in front of the camera," the frazzled mother says. "Do it again, David."

Just as the child attempts a step, Phillip decides to make a funny face into the camera.

Mother loses it. In her furor, she forgets to turn off the camera.

"You, over there!" she yells to one sidekick. "You, over there!" she says to the other, pointing in the opposite direction. "And don't move!"

"Robert, hold that baby up!"

"Everybody back off!" she says with a tone of insanity.

"Now, David. Walk!"

When Two Worlds Collide,
It Must Be 3 p.m.

It's 3 p.m. and my 13-year-old has just walked in the house after school.

3-year-old David runs to greet his "best friend."

"Hi Wobet!" David says, jumping into big brother's arms.

"Hi Davie!" Robert responds, turning the preschooler upside down.

It is both boys' favorite time of day. Robert, very glad to be home from school. David, elated to have a playmate.

Watching their antics with each other, I am struck by the differences between their lives.

Robert is in the awkward middle school years, quite possibly the worst years of a person's life.

David is in the carefree preschool years, quite possibly the best years of a person's life.

Robert gets up early and heads to school every day. The friendship jockeying and "fitting-in" issues greet him at the school doors.

When David gets up, he asks, "Do I go to school today?"

"School" for David is the house of a wonderful babysitter. He is greeted at the door by a small group of children jumping up and down, yelling, "Davie's here!"

Robert carries a big backpack, often filled with heavy schoolbooks.

David carries his own backpack. (Actually, it is an old swim bag. He doesn't mind the flowers on it.) It is filled with a bag of pretzels and a sippy cup.

Robert spends hours in the evening doing homework. Pre-algebra and accelerated reading requirements fill much of his free time.

David brings no homework from his "school." He has excelled in

"Truck Playing 101" and teeter-tottering.

Feeling left out, however, he has created his own version of homework.

"I'm going to do my work now," he has recently started saying.

His work involves a pair of child scissors and a piece of paper — sometimes two or three sheets. He cuts the paper into tiny pieces.

"Shhh!" he said the other evening. "I'm working." His tongue was sticking out to prove it.

Robert must concern himself with proficiency exams.

David does not even concern himself with staying in the lines of the coloring book.

Robert, as he has moved into his adolescence, has developed a belly. We have assured him that as he grows taller (Heaven forbid!) it will go away. He is self-conscious about it nonetheless.

David, as he has moved into his preschool years, takes great delight in emerging from the bathtub for a quick streak around the family room. He has absolutely no concept of self-consciousness.

Robert is concerned with his image. Only certain clothes are acceptable.

David is concerned with not putting both legs in one pant leg. After much struggle, he often ends up wearing the pants backward. (Which, to celebrate his independence, I find acceptable — depending on where we are going that day.)

Robert has begun weightlifting, hoping to gain strength and stamina for upcoming sports.

David, walking through the kitchen the other day, announced, "I'm sooo strong!" He is able to weightlift the world in his eyes.

Robert is nervous about baseball tryouts. He is diligently practicing his batting and catching.

David hits homeruns every time, in his imaginary world of living room baseball.

Robert is resistant to any form of affection. I have been relegated to a kiss on the forehead at bedtime.

David freely flows with affection. A big bear hug around the neck, kisses all over the face.

He is especially fond of giving and receiving raspberries on the belly.

Now that's something Robert remembers doing in those carefree preschool days. Those days, as he looks at his little brother, he often wishes he still lived in.

And that's what they are doing right now — at 3 p.m., after a long day at school, two "best friends" worlds apart, yet both "little" boys who want to be so very much like the other.

When Electric Bill Comes, Dad Gets a Shock

I don't think there is a father in America who hasn't given his children the "Dad doesn't own the electric company" speech.

My husband is no exception.

When the children were little, he tried gentle reasoning.

I remember one particular incident when Andrew was 3 years old.

He discovered that if he positioned himself a certain way on his bed, he could reach the light switch.

He took great joy in turning the light on and off in rapid succession.

As a busy mother of three young children, I felt it was a harmless pastime. It kept Andrew busy for a few minutes, until his little finger got tired.

Dad had a different opinion.

After being caught in the act one evening, he sat Andrew down for "the talk."

"Andrew, he began very calmly. "Daddy doesn't own the electric company…"

He paused to gauge Andrew's response — which was blank because he didn't know what electricity was.

"Every time you turn the light on, it costs Daddy a nickel," he continued.

"You don't want to cost Daddy lots of nickels, do you?" he asked, shaking his head.

The 3-year-old mimicked his father and shook his head.

"That's a good boy," Dad said, tapping Andrew on the head and getting up off the bed to leave the room.

"Daddy," Andrew said in his sweet, innocent voice. "Watch dis!"

He climbed back into position on his bed and began flicking the light on and off.

I thought the man was going to have a coronary.

As the children grew older, the gentle reasoning changed to hard-core shock treatment.

Come here, boys my husband called out one day after opening the electric bill.

"Daddy doesn't own the electric company," he began.

Immediately, dread ran through their bodies.

He took them outside to the new electric meter, which was new because he had convinced the electric company the old one *had* to be broken.

He made the children watch the dial go around.

Then, he sent one child inside.

"Turn on the computer!" he yelled.

They watched the dial.

"Now the TV!" he ordered next.

He went through every household device while the children stood "oohing" and "ahhing" at the dial.

I prayed he wouldn't call out "Clothes dryer!"

I knew for certain I would be picking him up off the ground.

The gas company has caused a great deal of strife in my husband's life as well.

The only thing in our house that runs on gas is our furnace.

Dad becomes highly irritated every summer when a gas bill arrives with a service charge for a service he isn't using.

One spring, he determined to end his frustration. He had the gas turned off.

"We won't need gas until the end of September!" he proclaimed.

It was a very cold September.

When he finally had the gas turned back on, the re-connection fee cost more than the amount he had saved on service charges.

The incident nearly gave him an ulcer.

He has finally experienced a momentary utility victory.

Last summer, he called a family meeting.

He was as proud as a peacock as he walked into the living room holding an envelope.

We all thought he had won the Publishers Clearing House Sweepstakes.

"Boys, I am proud of you," he said holding up the envelope. "This is the lowest electric bill we have ever had." His eyes swelled up with tears. "Thank you for listening to Dad."

I didn't have the heart to tell him that they had all been swimming a lot and not showering regularly.

The way the hot water heater makes the dial spin might just do him in.

Held Hostage

I was being held hostage in my car by a 4-year-old with a hose.

As I pulled into the driveway after work one hot afternoon, I saw my youngest child in the front lawn running around with the hose. I marveled at what great playmates a child and water are. I could see the smile on his face from the road. He was having a ball!

Stopping in front of the house, I leaned out the window to talk with the water squirter. He was soaking wet from head to toe. His shirt was off, lying in a wet puddle on the cement. His shorts were sagging from the weight of the water. His legs were covered in grass clippings, his toes brown with mud. Part of his hair was matted to his head, the rest was sticking out at various points, completely disheveled.

"Are you having fun?" I asked, knowing the answer.

At that moment, the cute, little, wet child transformed. The sweet, playful smile left his face, replaced by an evil, devilish grin.

I rolled up my window at lightning speed. Just as it reached the top, water pelted the glass.

He held the hose, pointed at the window for at least one full minute. Meanwhile, I scrambled around closing all other open windows.

When he stopped and the water had drained down the glass, I looked at him disapprovingly through the window. This prompted him to shoot the window again.

After the second barrage, I smiled nicely at the armed child and said, "Very funny, David. Now Mommy's going to get out of the car."

He shot the window again.

I crawled across the seat and started to open the door on the passenger side.

He shot over the car.

I paused to assess the situation. I had places to go this evening, so having my hair pelted with water would be a major inconvenience. Looking at my clothes, the skirt was cotton — no problem. My blouse, however, was dry clean only. A 10-yard dash into the house would cost me $10.50! I had come to a conclusion.

It was time to yell.

"David, put that hose down right now!" I yelled from my prison on wheels.

He stopped squirting. "What?" he asked.

"Drop the hose!" I yelled louder.

I believe he truly did not hear me the first time I yelled. But my incoherence gave his devilish mind an idea.

"What, Mom?" he asked again.

I fell for the ploy. I began rolling my window down to relay my harsh instructions. Luckily for me, his finger was trigger happy and he began squirting before I had the window down far enough to do any damage to my face.

I was now furious.

The car was becoming increasingly hotter. It was a stressful day at work. I had things to do in the house. I just wanted to get out of the car!

I laid my head on the steering wheel and pondered the reality that this child that I carried inside of me for nine long months — whose boo-boos I have kissed when he was hurt — whose hand I have held when he was scared — who has caused me more sleepless nights than I can count — is now holding me hostage with a hose!

Just as I was about to sink into deep despair, contemplating how I had come to this point in my life, I lifted my head and saw my 14-year-old walking out of the house.

Frantically, I waved and pointed.

"Get the hose!" I pleaded.

For a moment, I panicked. Robert could join forces with my captor. Together, they could hold me hostage indefinitely, making all sorts of demands — ice cream every night for dinner, a swimming pool in the back yard, no set bedtime, …

"No," I thought. He didn't come out to join forces. He wants something from me. I was safe.

Robert, however, was not.

He quickly analyzed the situation and in his best big-brother voice, addressed the 4-year-old.

"David, put down the hose," he said sternly.

David looked at his big brother. He adores Robert and for a moment, the sweet, innocent smile returned to the child's face.

Then feeling the hot handle of the squirter, the devil grin reappeared.

Robert saw it the same time I did.

"Don't squirt me!" he began yelling. "David, I mean…" His voice became garbled as water filled his mouth.

David squirted him from head to toe.

After a short struggle, Robert retrieved the hose from the devil child and I got out of the car.

Angrily, we looked at the 4-year-old who, without his hose, looked sweet and innocent again.

"Clean yourself off and come in the house," I ordered.

"OK," he said with remorse in his voice.

After changing my clothes, I looked out the kitchen window to check on the child's progress.

Indeed, he looked much cleaner. The mud was washed from his feet. The grass was gone from his legs.

In fact, I could tell he was cleaner from head to toe, as he stood cleaning his shorts — which he was holding in his hands.

Lessons of the Lemonade Stand

God bless everyone who has ever stopped at a lemonade stand!

I believe there is a special place in heaven for people who have paid hot, sweaty and most likely dirty children they do not know for a drink they do not really want.

Children selling lemonade may be the most pitifully endearing sight on the face of the earth.

Every summer, the three families of children who make up our small neighborhood determine to strike it rich in the lemonade business.

They drag the child-size picnic table out to the road.

They make a big, unreadable sign.

Never having fresh lemons, they mix a powder brand with water and stir.

Then, they wait.

Living on a country road where the speed limit is supposed to be 35 but is seldom obeyed, the wait can be very long.

Baseball games and squirt-gun fights erupt during the wait.

This makes the lemonade stand workers thirsty. So, they drink the lemonade.

One hot, summer day, three gallons of lemonade disappeared before one customer was served.

Being entrepreneurs, the neighborhood clan is always coming up with new ways to serve the public.

One year, along with the lemonade, they sold "mud balls" and "Indian feathers." Signs were made and a display of these products was laid next to the lemonade.

They never sold a mud ball or a feather. If I recall correctly, it was a very slow lemonade day. The two product lines just didn't mesh.

Another year, they decided to sell candy bars for a dollar with a free glass of lemonade. This concept went like gangbusters! They sold 36 bars!

(I had been away this day and couldn't believe all they had sold. My husband explained that there had been several friends who had stopped. I suspect a neighborhood mom had been on the phone!)

Unfortunately, the candy bars were for a fund-raising effort, and they each cost a dollar. Success had eluded their grasp again.

Recently, one warm Friday evening, the neighborhood gang set up shop again.

They pulled the picnic table out to the road, made their unreadable sign and stirred up some Kool-Aid. (I wasn't ready for lemonade season yet!)

Then they waited.

I sat on the front porch watching their excitement rise at the sight of a car on the horizon and then fall as the car drove on by.

So pitiful and yet...

I stepped into the house to refresh my drink. I looked out the window and all five boys were going crazy in the yard.

Grant had his hands up in the air. Phillip was jumping up and down. Caleb was holding his stomach. Andrew was giving David a high five.

"What happened?" I asked.

"He gave us $2!" one yelled.

"He didn't even want a drink!" another said.

Apparently, 3-year-old David had been crawling around on the picnic table and fell off as this car drove by.

The man turned around and came back.

"He said it was great Friday night entertainment!" the boys informed me.

That man has no idea the joy his $2 provided five little boys.

Later than evening, another customer stopped and paid 50 cents for his 25-five-cent drink of warm Kool-Aid.

Thanks to these Samaritans, each child made 50 cents that evening, which ended up in the gum-ball machines on their next trip to the grocery store.

I believe the boys know that their lemonade is truly nothing to stop for. I think they understand that there is a pity factor involved with every customer.

I believe they also know that every person who stops to buy their stirred-up powder mix in a cup is a kind, generous, caring individual who took the time to make them feel special.

They need to know there are people like that.

It may be one of the best lessons they will ever learn for 25 cents.

It's Official: My Mind Has Turned Into Jelly

I made a jelly and jelly sandwich this morning.

The peanut butter was sitting on the counter right next to the bread. I never saw it or even contemplated using it.

As I stared at the two slices of bread smeared with grape jelly, the realization hit me.

I have completely lost my mind.

It's been coming on for quite some time, the slow deterioration of my brain cells causing confusion, culminating to this point when I cannot even make a peanut butter and jelly sandwich.

I believe I started losing my mind after my first child was born. I did the usual silly things that a new mother does. I walked out of the house with my slippers on. I showed up at church with all my makeup on, except for the blush because the baby started to cry and I forgot to go back into the bathroom and apply the color to my cheeks. I went to the store with the baby, the stroller, the diaper bag and toy bag, but not my purse.

The day I gave the baby the coffee and my husband the pacifier, we began to suspect a serious loss of mind.

Even that was dismissed as through the years, with more children arriving in our household, I began calling them the wrong names. My misnaming used to garner a rise out of my children. Now, they just roll their eyes, figure out which one I am really trying to talk to, and respond. My youngest child will answer to anything as long as I am looking at him and speaking.

But even my misnaming has gotten progressively worse through the years. Once, I was looking at my child, running down through the names of all the children trying to address this particular one, and the dog's name slipped into the list.

My son was appalled. I tried to explain to him that I said the dog's name because the dog was the reason I was calling him. I wanted the child to feed the dog. Instead, my son thought that I thought that he was the dog.

"She thinks I'm the dog," he announced to his brothers.

After he relayed the story, the boys immediately consoled him with reassurances that his mother truly does not think he is the dog. "It's just mom," they said with their fingers going in circles around their ears.

I could justify this morning's jelly and jelly incident: It's too early to be making sandwiches... I was actually going to make two sandwiches... I believe peanuts make you nuts... (Maybe that's my problem!) But an incident a week before the jelly and jelly has brought me to the conclusion that I am becoming dangerously brain numb.

We were sitting at a freshman football game. One of the mothers had to go to a meeting and asked me if I would take her son Ben home after the game.

"No problem," I told her. But there was a problem. I have no mind.

After the game, I picked up my son, gathered the other two boys from their practice and headed home. Fifteen minutes after we were home, Robert was talking about his team.

"We have a great line," he was saying. "Me, Kyle, Chris, Ben..."

My hands went up in the air waving frantically as I screamed, "Ben! Ben! Oh my God! I forgot Ben!" I ran out to the van, still screaming, still waving my arms frantically.

(It was a panic I had not felt since my fourth child was a baby and I pulled out of the driveway and left him sitting on the kitchen table in his car seat.)

I backed out of the driveway at Mach speed and raced down the road. My family stood at the door, their mouths open with a queer, questioning look on their faces. They thought I had gone completely insane. They, of course, knew nothing of my promise to bring this child home. If they had known, *they* would have remembered.

I found Ben safe at home. He had called his dad after the game. I apologized profusely. They assured me my blunder had caused no harm.

Forgetting to buy milk is harmless. Forgetting to take out the trash on garbage day is somewhat offensive, but forgivable. Forgetting someone's child is an inexcusable act of mindlessness.

This morning, when I announced the jelly and jelly situation, I saw the boys nod knowingly to one another.

They've been telling me I've been losing my mind for years. Between Ben and the jelly, they knew it had finally taken its leave. Robert came up behind me and put his hand on my shoulder.

"I don't like the peanut butter anyway," he said with a kind, sympathetic tone.

I looked at him with a pathetic stare of befuddlement. "Thank you, (pause) son."

We both knew I couldn't remember his name just then.

Mud Puddle or Cool Pool?

Easy Choice

We have a swimming pool in our back yard.

This spring, my husband spent the better part of a week hooking up hoses, going to the pool store and making adjustments to get the pool up and running.

I, too, have spent time at the pool store buying chemicals and discussing problems. I check the water every day and add chemicals a couple of times a week.

Hours and hours have been spent sweeping and skimming the surface.

I was thrilled this past weekend when the gray clouds finally lifted and the sun was shining bright.

"I am putting on my bathing suit and going out to the pool for the whole day!" I announced at breakfast.

The boys thought that sounded like a good idea. They and a couple of their friends, along with my niece, put on their bathing suits and headed outside.

They never made it to the pool.

They spent the entire afternoon playing in the mud puddle that the rain had made at the bottom of our yard.

I sat in total, utter disbelief, sunning myself on the pool deck.

When I first heard them over by the puddle, I opened one eye and peered out. They were timidly sticking their toes in the water.

After chasing a frog through the puddle, all hesitance was gone. They started stomping through the muddy water, racing each other from side to side. They kicked, screamed, laughed and splashed, each one trying to outdo the other's water antics.

Then came the ultimate double-dog-dare challenge: Run and slide face first into the puddle.

"Go get the video camera," they yelled over to me, hoping to save this moment for posterity.

I wanted to tell them what I would like to do with that video camera. I didn't. It wouldn't have mattered anyway. They would never have heard me over all the cheers and hollers as the first daredevil's face slid into the water.

One by one, they slammed their bodies onto the ground and smashed into the mud. Rising out of the water from their feat, they each looked like the Creature from the Black Lagoon. But they wiped the mud from their eyes and got in line to do it again.

When my niece stood poised, ready to run headfirst into the puddle, I knew the mud puddle had created an uncontrollable crazed frenzy.

Meanwhile, I sat by the nice, clear, chemically balanced water in the pool and wondered why I had wasted my time keeping it that way. If they liked brown, muddy water, surely a green, algae-infested pool would be a blast.

It reminded me of the year we bought the boys bikes for Christmas.

In an effort to heighten the suspense of the gifts, I made three trips to a local appliance store to get refrigerator boxes to hide the bikes. Christmas morning, the boys couldn't wait to see what was inside the big boxes, but we made them open their other gifts first.

Turns out, it didn't matter what was inside the boxes. The bikes sat by the Christmas tree until — two weeks later — the boxes had been worn out by the boys.

I remember sitting with my husband by the tree, looking at all the presents that were being ignored while the boys played in, around, over and under the boxes. We wondered why we had spent a dime on any of it.

That's how I felt as I sat by the pool this day. I refused to let myself add up the cost to run this bucket of water. My mind started calculating anyway.

Luckily, the kids came running up to the deck and interrupted my thoughts.

"Whoa! You're not jumping into this pool like that!" I yelled just in time as one of the mud-laden lagoon monsters was about to jump into my crystal clear water.

"Go wash off with the hose!" I ordered all of them.

That was the closest they got to the pool that day. The rest of the afternoon was spent running around and squirting each other with our $10 hose.

Christmas Memories are the Most Cherished Gifts

I collect Nativity scenes. So, every year around Christmas, there is a smattering of the holy scene in various forms throughout the house.

About three years ago, I started finding the individual pieces to the scenes moved, after I had painstakingly placed each one just right.

The modus operandi was always the same. Mary and Joseph would be pushed right up against the baby in the manger. If the scene included the shepherd boy or the wise men, they also would be smashed up against the manger, encircling it.

Every time I came across this irritation, which was daily, I would impatiently move the figures back to where they "belonged."

Finally, I could not take this any longer. In my most anti-Christmas voice, I demanded to know who the culprit was.

Andrew, 4 years old at the time, sheepishly stepped forward to take the blame.

"Why are you doing this?" I demanded.

With tears in his eyes he said, "I just want baby Jesus to be warm."

My heart pierced with selfish guilt, together we went and put the nativity scenes the "right" way — Andrew's way.

Through the years he has added a new twist to his nativity trimming. He turns baby Jesus around to face Mary and Joseph.

I don't change one.

I have found that the things I remember and cherish most about Christmas are not the presents and surprise gifts I have received. In fact, I remember more presents that I was excited about giving than ones I received. What I remember most are the people I have spent Christmas with and the things we have done together.

As a child, I remember dancing to Christmas songs around the tree; making a special trip to the big downtown "fancy" store to shop; counting houses decorated in lights; going to Grandma's on Christmas Eve; listening for reindeer hooves.

As a parent, there are a host of Christmas memories that I will cherish forever. Each one, a gift in and of itself.

Although Christmas day has not yet arrived this year, I have already added a new memory to my list of those to cherish forever.

Every year, when the Christmas toy catalog arrives, the boys devour each page with circles and stars, noting everything they want. (I have often felt it would be simpler and neater for them to mark all those things they do NOT want.) Every page is filled with their markings.

This year, Phillip, 9, and Andrew, 7, went a step further.

For three evenings, they sat next to each other on the couch — one holding the catalog, the other a pencil and paper.

They went through each page, discussing every toy and writing down their choices.

"You like this one?" one would say.

"Oh yeah!" the other would respond. "Do you?"

"Sure. Hey, maybe David would like that too."

"OK. Write it down and put a three beside it."

Occasionally, they would yell for Robert, not sure if they should mark down an item for him.

David, being small, was never consulted, although he was not over-looked.

When I received their two-column, one-and-a-half page list, I didn't know whether to laugh or cry.

It was completely unreasonable for them to think they would receive all these toys, but their eyes were filled with confident expectation.

As I read through the list, detailing their desires for one of this and four of that, I found they hadn't left anybody out. It was complete with a tool set for Dad and a dish set for Mom.

No gift under the tree this Christmas could be more special than my starred and circled "dish set" from the toy catalog.

Little Man is in a Big Hurry
to Grow Up

David was standing in the busy amusement park thoroughfare eating a corn dog as fast as he could chew.

As he swallowed the last gulp, he stood as tall as he could up against his big brother and asked, "Now how tall am I?"

It was an endearing sight and yet so heart wrenching.

All day, this child of 39 inches had been looking at roller coasters and thrill rides that "go up to the sky." How he longed to go on those rides.

"You're not tall enough," we told him over and over again, being careful not to say "not big enough." David contends he IS big.

He thought if he stuffed down a corn dog really fast, it would put him over the top of the height requirement.

I didn't have the heart to tell him he probably wouldn't be tall enough to ride next year either.

Ironically, by the time he is tall enough, common sense will have settled in his now-fearless brain and he may be too afraid to ride these rides he longs for.

"How many days will I go to school?" David asked me for the thousandth time during the last week of summer vacation.

"Two days," I told him again.

"How many days does Robert go to school?" he wanted to know.

"Five days," I explained.

David's little mind could not understand this injustice.

"But I have a backpack!" he exclaimed.

In his 4-year-old mind, having a backpack like a big boy meant he should go to school as many days as the big boys.

If he only knew that all his brothers would be happy to trade their five days for his two.

"I want to sweep," David pleaded with me as I vacuumed the floor.

"I think the sweeper will be too heavy for you to push," I told him.

He tried with all his might but could barely budge the bulky vacuum. I suggested we vacuum together but his pride had been hurt and he no longer wanted to.

I know that when he is old enough to easily maneuver the sweeper, he will grumble over the chore.

"No, you may not go on a bike ride with your brothers," I said to David, still in shock that he can even ride a bike at his age.

"But I'm 4 years old!" he insisted, holding up four fingers proudly.

"When you are this many, you can go for a bike ride on the road," I explained to him, unfolding all his fingers.

His face fell in complete disbelief. In his mind, it would be *forever* before he was all those fingers old.

Standing there, holding his little hands, I was experiencing my own disbelief.

It seemed like just yesterday I was holding this little man in my arms.

It will seem like tomorrow when it will take all his fingers to count his age.

That leaves me with today.

So when David wants to play, I put down the dish towel, sit on the floor and build a tower for him to knock over.

"You are so strong," I say.

"Strong like Robert?" he asks.

"Oh yes," I respond.

When David wants to read, I put down my book and pick up *The Cat in the Hat.*

We read it together. David knows all the words.

"You are so smart," I tell him.

"Smart like Phillip?" he wonders.

"Absolutely," I assure him.

When it is nap time, I set aside the laundry basket and lie down with him, holding his hand and tickling his belly with the other.

He curls up giggling, then attacks back, waving his arms wildly to distract my attention.

"You're funny," I laugh.

"Funny like Andrew?" he giggles back.

"Yes, and goofy too." I tickle him again.

This child, so determined to "be big" and keep up with his brothers, has no idea how perfect his world is right now.

But tomorrow, when his wish is granted and he is "big" like his brothers — and bigger still — it will be today that he looks back on and wishes for.

Cleanliness is Sometimes Next to Impossible

"If it takes you more than a split second to answer the question, 'When was the last time you took a shower?' it has been too long!" I said, addressing my children during a recent family meeting.

The meeting had been called because the shower question had been asked of two children whose prolonged response, with their eyes rolled back in their head to consider the answer to the question, caused great angst in the life of their mother.

After pondering the question intensely, one child had answered, "I don't know…"

The other, noting my response to the first, answered promptly, "Two days ago."

He quickly learned that was the wrong answer as well.

At first, I lamented the fact that I, once again, needed to make yet another rule about yet another seemingly common sense issue.

Then, in my usual motherly fashion, I laid a guilt trip upon myself for obviously not teaching my children proper hygiene.

After analyzing (and overanalyzing) the situation, I have determined that boys from the age of 8 to 11 are in stench denial.

My 4-year-old loves to take a bath. A tub of water, a few suds and some toys and he is one happy boy! He won't come out until he's wrinkly and squeaky clean.

I can't get my 14-year-old out of the shower. "Long and often" seems to be his motto. Every time I turn around, he's under the water. I have had to talk with him about showering less often and with more speed.

My 9- and 11-year-olds could be standing in front of me with mud caked on their extremities and every strand of hair matted to their heads and ask "Why?" when told to take a shower.

You would think looking at each other would be a hint! Apparently, dirt reflects clean.

Our first conversation about shower habits occurred after laundry day one week.

As the piles of clothes for each child were stacked high, I noticed a lack of white in the 9- and 11-year-olds' piles. Calling them to the sorting table, I accused them of not putting their dirty clothes in the hamper.

"Go get them," I ordered, envisioning a mound of dirty clothes under the bed.

They came back empty handed, proud that they had not been neglectful.

"To the shower!" I yelled in horror as the reality hit me. The pride washed from their faces — with soap and water.

Soap is another rule I have had to enforce. It seems standing under the water for 10 minutes denotes clean to a pre-teen.

I actually have to say, "Go take a shower and use soap." When they are done, I follow up with, "Did you use soap?" just to be sure.

Once, after I noticed a lack of body and bounce in my child's hair, he exclaimed, "Well, we haven't had any shampoo for a week!"

They tell me when they are hungry. They tell me every new toy and video game they want. They don't tell me when they need shampoo and soap to clean their bodies.

I have found a way to solve this dilemma. I always know when the boys have soap and are actually using the soap because the 14-year-old will yell about it.

"WHY do you always leave the soap on the shower floor?" the clean brother will demand. "And why do you always break it into little pieces?"

This is a major peeve of the 14-year-old. He seethes over broken soap. Which may be why the 9- and 11-year-olds break it.

I believe however, it is simply their way of conquering the whole shower routine. If they have to be clean, by god they are going to make the soap pay.

I have seen it broken into little pieces. I have seen it with a hole bored through the middle of it. I have seen it with chunks knocked out of the ends. They work hard at mutilating the soap.

Come to think of it: All that soap mutilation has got to take a long time. The next time they are done with a shower I better ask, "Did you *use* soap on your *body*?"

Fun Meal: $1.99; Shoes: $40;

Kids' Smiles: Priceless

We had been shopping and it was lunch time, so I took my 4-year-old out to eat.

As I placed his fun meal in front of him, his eyes lit up. Quickly, he dug to the bottom of the bag. He squealed with delight as he pulled out the toy from inside.

Sitting there watching him, I became amazed at what $1.99 had just bought.

A hamburger (ketchup only), a bag of fries, fruit punch and a 10-cent toy in exchange for a smile that lights up my world from a child who thinks I'm the greatest for buying him this special treat.

A million dollars could not have made either one of us happier.

On the other hand, when shopping with my 14-year-old, a million dollars is not nearly enough — no smile included.

"I *have* to have these shoes," he told me with a look of agonizing pain on his face.

For a moment, I stared at him. His expression was so full of anguish and despair he looked as if he were completely shoeless. I looked down at his feet. He was not shoeless. His feet were clad in a perfectly fine pair of shoes.

Looking at the pair he "needed" so desperately, I couldn't believe my eyes.

"They look like clown shoes," I told him.

He rolled his eyes. I am *so* not cool.

Rubbing my hands along the inside I observed, "There is no arch support."

More rolling.

"They're $40," I announced a little too loudly, reading the price tag on the bottom. "Take the star off the side and this is a $5 pair of shoes!"

His look of despair turned to agony as my words fell on his ears.

"Want a hamburger?" I asked as we walked out of the store.

"No," he pouted in return.

$1.99 wasn't about to make him happy.

But some hard work did.

He helped his father at work and saved up babysitting money. In less than a month, Robert had $50. We returned to the store for those shoes that he "needed."

He stared at the clown shoes a little longer than he did the day he expected me to buy them.

In the end, he decided he did indeed need them. Hesitantly, he laid his hard-earned money on the counter.

Carrying his bag out of the store, he complained about the tax. "Why is it so much?" he wanted to know. He had never noticed tax before.

I looked at him as he walked to the car with a smile covering his face.

His smile lit up my world, just like the smile of my 4-year-old.

Yet, this 14-year-old's smile was different. It wasn't a smile brought on by delight over a treat that had been bought for him. It wasn't a smile of adoration for me as the giver of the treat.

His smile was personal. It caused him to walk a little taller and hold his head up a little higher for what he had accomplished.

He wanted something. He worked hard and saved his money for it. Now he was holding his treasure in his hands.

For a moment, I felt a tinge of regret. Being the hero with the goodies is a big thrill for me as a parent.

But if I had bought those shoes for him, in my giving, I would have robbed my son of a gift that he will carry with him long after his prized shoes are worn out.

Pride and self-respect cannot be given. They must be earned.

Robert's price for earning his self-respect and pride was hard work and $40 (plus tax).

What he received for that price was a pair of cherished shoes and a smile of self-satisfaction. That smile is priceless.

I will continue to surprise my 4-year-old with $1.99 treats. Yet, I know there will come a time when he will no longer squeal with delight over the toy at the bottom of the bag.

He will long for his heart's desire (hopefully the clown shoe phase will have passed). He will work and save and buy his treasure.

He too, will walk with pride and smile a smile that money can't buy.

A Very Bad Idea

The stories are a bit conflicting about whose bright idea it was to put my mother on a pair of ice skates.

My mother insists it was my father. "He kept telling me to put the skates on."

My father says he told her he thought it was NOT a good idea. "But she wanted to try," he says with a sigh of resignation.

My sister was present for the debacle. "Why didn't you stop her?" I asked, incredulously.

"She walks with a cane," I said slowly, trying to impress upon all of them the utter insanity of this idea.

Mom attempted the ice-skating feat on a Sunday afternoon. Her surgery was Monday.

The fall severed the bone in her forearm.

"They said she will need some pins and nuts and bolts and stuff," my father said when he called late Sunday evening to inform me of the "accident."

I laid awake much of the night struggling with whether my mother had a death wish or my family was trying to kill her.

I was still debating the issue when I arrived at my parents' house Monday. But Mom was in pretty good spirits and was most upset about "all this fuss over a broken arm."

"How far did you skate?" I asked Mom as she sat in the living room before heading to the hospital for surgery, her bandaged forearm resting on a pillow.

She opened her mouth to answer and then closed it abruptly and shook her head. It seems she didn't quite have the blades under her feet for any amount of time.

When my sister and father took her to the emergency room the night before, a nurse had asked why she had grass stains on her knees. Apparently, she had trouble getting to the lake in the backyard and crawled a good bit of the way.

"This was a sign," I informed them all. They all agreed. Then my sister began to giggle, remembering the look on the nurse's face when she found out Mom had ice skates on when she "slipped on the ice." Apparently, Mom had left out some of the details of her fall.

The giggle turned into a chuckle when we arrived at the hospital Monday afternoon. April dropped Mom and me off at the front door while she parked the car.

Mom started in through the revolving door.

I thought she might have difficulty pushing the door, so I hopped in behind her.

I thought wrong.

Truly, the space allotted in revolving doors is for one person only. Breathing down my mother's neck, we shuffled around and then stopped.

I was carrying my purse, my work bag, my mother's purse and her overnight bag. My mother's purse did not make it.

Stuck between the inside and the outside, this "Laurel and Hardy" mother-daughter duo attempted to back up in the revolving door.

After several minutes of bumping, pushing and smooshing, I pulled the purse through and we shuffled around inside. We were laughing so hard we were barely able to tell the registration desk attendant who we were.

We fell into hysterics in the waiting room when the doctor came to get Mom's medical history.

"Diabetes?" he asked.

"No," Mom replied.

"Heart disease?"

"No," Mom answered again.

"Any previous surgeries?" the doctor continued.

"No," Mom said, very matter-of-fact.

Luckily, my sister and I were listening.

"Mom," we said, looking at her in amazement. "You had brain surgery."

"Oh yeah!" she said in surprise, looking at the doctor. "I did. I had brain surgery."

The doctor looked at her as if perhaps she needed another one.

He soon realized that it runs in the family. When the nurse arrived to take Mom into surgery, she instructed her, "Leave your glasses here."

"Better talk loud," my sister said to the nurse. "She can't hear without them."

Home is Where My Heart Is, so Buyer has to be Just Right

"What did they think of the place?" my husband asked after a pro-spective buyer left our home.

"It wasn't for them," I responded.

"Really?" he asked, a bit surprised at such a direct response. "Is that what they said?"

"Well, not exactly," I answered, a bit sheepishly. "I told them it wasn't for them."

"You did what?"

"Their children are all older," I justified. "Who would play in the little cubby hole in the family room?"

He stared at me with a look I had never seen before. I couldn't tell if he was mad or confused, or if he thought I was wise or completely out of my mind.

Moving seemed like a great idea at first. We had found a home with several acres, a pool and a lake all at a price we couldn't pass up. It fit all the qualifications of our dreams. The children thought they had just found heaven.

But as I began packing all our belongings into boxes to move, I found myself filled with bittersweet emotions over leaving this house that has been our home for 10 years.

It started in the dining room, as I packed the china. A decade of Thanksgiving and Christmas dinners have been spent in this room. The first year, I had no clue what I was doing. My two brothers-in-law arrived at 5 a.m. to help me prepare the turkey. Now I have holiday dinners down to a science. I grew up a lot in this dining room.

This dining room has watched my children grow up as well. My third son, Andrew, celebrated his first birthday surrounded by these walls. We sang "Happy Birthday" three times because he liked blowing out the candle so much. By the time he became tired of blowing, we had to scrape the icing off the top of the cake. One-year-olds blow more than air.

My bittersweet emotions continued as I packed the living room. We spent many cold winter evenings huddled around the fireplace in this room. There is a burn mark on the carpet to prove it.

These walls have heard many chapters of books, read aloud to the children. They have heard my deepest thoughts and prayers on those nights when sleep eluded me. They have heard the laughter and tears of friends visiting for the evening or stopping by for tea in the afternoon.

As I packed the family room, I smiled for the first time at the French doors leading to the back yard. Soon after they were built, our dog scratched the wood, trying to get outside and play with the kids. The first time I saw the marks, I thought my heart had stopped. Now, they seemed to give the room character and I became a bit possessive. Those were *our* marks from *our* dog.

Even one of our bathrooms brought a feeling of melancholy to me. We remodeled this bath three times, and we still had to bring in a professional to make some repairs before we moved. This room has always been a sore reminder to my husband and me of our ineptitude at home improvements. Looking at it now, completely unrecognizable from the day we moved in, I felt proud of our accomplishment.

Tears flowed from my eyes as I packed David's bedroom. We brought David home from the hospital to this room. I remember the day. Every child in the neighborhood came over to see him. They stared in awe at his little face and hands. He was a novelty.

And he still is. He has his own food cupboard at a neighbor's house. The second he walks through the door Mrs. Crider asks, "Are you hungry?" He heads for the cupboard to see what goodies she stocked for him.

I can't even think of leaving the neighbors of this home without crying. There is no way to calculate the value of good neighbors.

The older children of the neighborhood have all taken turns babysitting my children. The younger ones seem more like an extension of our family.

So you see, I can't sell this house to just anybody. I have to sell my home to the perfect family who will create more memories within these walls and complete the neighborhood.

After all Andrew had his first haircut in this back yard...

Robert stood at the end of the driveway and caught the school bus to go to his first day of kindergarten...

Phillip learned to ride a bike on this grass...

The World Opens Up When the Video Games are Closed

It's official. My husband and I are "the meanest parents in the world."

This distinction was bestowed upon us one day last week. My husband arrived home from work early on a beautiful, sunny fall day to find two of our children glued in front of the television playing PlayStation.

They learned quickly that the proper response to "Turn it off!" is not "I just want to beat this level first."

The PlayStation was unhooked and "put away."

It's been "put away" before, but somehow, they knew this time was different. Dad had reached his last "level."

The outcry was horrific. You would think we had just cut off their thumbs, which would be a shame since that is the most physically fit part of their bodies.

Our oldest son handled the news about the removal of the system the best. At 14, he is fairly busy with other interests. In defense of the weekend nights he likes to stay up late playing, he insisted, "I have to use my brain more playing those games than I do at school."

My husband and I looked at each other in amazement. We had no idea "007" required more brain power than algebra. We figure now that he won't be spending his weekends calculating the venue of bad guys, he will have lots of brain power to calculate x times y, which should equal all "A's."

We found our youngest son's reaction to the game system's being put away almost comical, "This is the worst day ever," he moped with a fake cry in his voice. For my husband and I, we figured a fake cry was better than the real tears he has cried waiting for his turn to play.

The two who had been caught playing PlayStation on a sunny day were near devastation. Their faces had the strangest expressions: a mixture between a scowl and complete, utter disbelief. Their mouths hung half-open for an entire day. They didn't really say anything initially, but they looked like they wanted to say something. In their devastation, they just couldn't find the words. Their thumbs twitched, uncontrollably.

"Go outside and play!" became our parental mantra.

That first day they had been ordered outdoors, we found our 10-year-old standing in the driveway, peering in through the window at the television and the empty spot where the PlayStation once sat. Tears were streaming down his face.

My husband saw him first. To his credit, he turned and walked away. With fire in his eyes, he told me what the child was doing.

"He needs a chore," I responded.

He spent the next hour cleaning the bathroom and his bedroom. He hasn't cried over the PlayStation since.

The second day, the boys found their voice.

"This is so dumb!... We don't play it that much!... Everybody else plays a lot more than we do!..." That's the day we were dubbed "the meanest parents in the world."

We told them to go tell the world — while playing outside.

Their day consisted of a football game, with Dad as the quarterback. They invented some "survivor" game, involving climbing trees. After dark, a heated contest of Capture the Flag.

By the third evening, I had to tell them to come in to get ready for bed.

I HAD TO TELL THEM TO COME IN TO GET READY FOR BED!

That's when I knew they were right. We are the meanest parents in the world.

It is downright cruel and unusual punishment to have let them play those silly video games in the first place! They have missed countless evenings making leaf piles, playing "hide from the cars" and creating forts.

I wonder how many times I could have whipped them in "Sorry" if they hadn't been playing video games?

Being "the meanest" is a little more time consuming than being nice — and a lot louder.

When they are not sitting in a vegetative state in front of a video screen, they tend to make a ruckus. They also tend to want you to play with them.

More time together with our loud, lively kids...

Well, we may very well end up being "the meanest parents in the universe."

I think the PlayStation shelf will remain empty for a while.

Maker of the Universe vs Maker
of the Lunches

It was a Sunday morning and I had gone in to wake the children three times. The last time, I could hear them conspiring in whispered voices as I entered the room.

"Get up and get ready for church!" I yelled, in a less than holy voice.

Normally, I don't even have to wake the children on Sunday morning. My children simply do not know the meaning of sleeping in. On the few occasions I do need to wake them, one call is always enough.

But the children were scheming this Sunday morning. As I was busy getting ready to go worship the God in heaven, all hell was about to break loose.

I reverted to insisting that my husband go in and get them moving. He informed me he was not going to yell this morning.

"We'll go to church ourselves," he said.

I was not happy about this. In fact, I was mad as... well, suffice it to say, I was boiling.

As we were walking out the door, I could not resist one last jab at the fake sleepers.

"If you don't have time for the Maker of the Universe," I informed them, "I don't have time for you."

It was my attempt at a hellfire and brimstone one-sentence sermon.

The point of my anger was two-fold. First, in our family, church is required attendance as much as school or work. Sure, we miss Sundays, just as we are absent from our weekday obligations occasionally. I do not think my children will go to hell by missing one day of services. But their behavior was blatant disobedience, and I wasn't about to tolerate it.

Second, as I reminded them later, two hours on a Sunday morning is not asking too much for the Maker of the Universe.

When my husband and I arrived home from church, the children were flushed in the face. They had been outside chopping wood.

Apparently, they thought firewood was proper penance. Their father was impressed. I was unforgiving.

I stuck to my guns. They didn't have time for the Maker, I didn't have time for them.

They got their own lunch.

They made their own dinner.

Dad suggested they pack their lunches for school the next day.

"I don't think your mother is going to do it for you," he told them.

Monday morning, I didn't "have time" to wake them up. They all missed the school bus.

Before their father took them to school, I sat them down on the couch.

"You think you know what's best for you?" I continued my fire and brimstone sermon. "You have proven that you don't."

You would think I would have been in my glory. Taking care of myself was definitely easier than doing for the whole family. But by Monday afternoon, I felt like a louse. I was completely derelict of my motherly duties. I didn't know how much longer I could "not have time" for my children.

Then Andrew arrived home from school.

"Mom, will you wake me up tomorrow morning? If I'm late again, I'll get a detention."

"Will you listen and obey this Sunday morning?"

"Yes," he assured me.

Phillip asked if I would "please" pack his lunch tomorrow morning.

I made the same Sunday morning deal with him.

By evening, we were back to normal. Dinner was made, lunches were packed, there was help with homework.

I was pleased with the way "making time for the Maker of the

Universe" had played out. They all learned a valuable lesson.

But "the Maker" had one lesson left. This one was for me. Truly, there is a consequence for every action.

When I dropped David off at preschool the next day, the teacher pulled me aside.

"We gave David a hamburger for lunch yesterday," she informed me in a hushed voice. "He had only an apple and six pieces of candy in his lunch."

Life Lessons Learned on My Kitchen Table

I was wiping off the kitchen table for what seemed like the hundredth time today.

With the children home all day for the holidays, it seems one of them is hungry all the time.

My mind wandered aimlessly while performing this mundane task, and I wondered to myself how many times I had wiped this table clean — thousands, maybe hundreds of thousands of times.

As I began calculating numbers in my head, my thoughts were interrupted by what my eyes witnessed beneath my dishcloth.

There were marks and scars and gashes all over the table's surface.

This table was bought less than two years ago. It replaced an old, "inherited" table that we had used for years.

I remember how thrilled I was with the table when we brought it into the house. I vowed to take perfect care of it.

Looking at its marred surface, I realized my vow had been broken.

There is a large area near the center of the table where the varnish is removed. This mark appeared not long after the table arrived.

Phillip had spent some of his birthday money on a Snoopy snow cone machine. I remember driving him home from the store. He was so excited to make the frosty, flavored treats.

He and brother Andrew and a neighbor friend crushed ice with the machine and poured toppings on the ice. They crushed and laughed and ate for hours.

When they were done, they left the snow cone machine sitting on the table. The remnants of ice left in it dripped out onto the new table and stained the varnish.

That was stain number one. I was very upset when I saw it.

Other stains appeared gradually.

White glue spots are found near the edge of one side of the table from Andrew building his Cub Scout Rain Gutter Regatta boat. It is hard to keep glue from dripping off the protective newspaper covering when you are so intent on creating a winning vessel.

Then, gash marks are strategically placed on the table in front of where each chair sits. These are remnants of David's Play-Doh adventures. He has created and cut-up more snakes and pizza pies on that table than can be counted.

The gash marks are made more noticeable by the dull areas that mysteriously appear in those areas in front of the chairs as well. Many bowls of cereal have been consumed in those dull areas. Much milk has been spilled to create the lackluster look.

Just as I was finishing my wiping task, I noticed a new set of marks on the table. Thin lines circling the entire circumference of the table — eight or ten of them, going around and around.

"I saw David playing with his car on the table," Robert suggested as he saw me looking at the marks.

I rubbed with the dishcloth. The lines did not come off.

Once again, I could feel my blood starting to boil as I thought about still another mark ruining my precious table.

But as I walked to the sink, a realization about the table hit me.

This place where my family sits together to eat and laugh and share stories of their day, by its imperfections, is becoming a legacy of our life.

Every mark is a story. Each gash is a memory.

My preoccupation with perfection caused me to miss the beauty of each imperfection.

The faults in my kitchen table have given it great personality and character — features it would not have if it were still perfect.

Life is like my kitchen table.

We want our lives to be perfect and unblemished, but it is in the spills, messes and gashes of living that we build our character and personality.

As we celebrate a new year, I wish you much happiness and joy.

But also, may your year be filled with just enough spilled milk and glue spots to create marks of character and personality in you — a living legacy that cannot be wiped away.

Kids Supervise Themselves

I phoned home to check on the kids while I was at work.

"Hello," a shy voice answered.

"Andrew?" I guessed correctly. He is the only child I know who sounds homeless when he answers the phone at home.

"What are you doing?" I ask.

"Well, I'm just sitting here right now," he said, sounding pathetic, which I ignored.

"Where is Robert?" I continued.

"He's sleeping," the 9-year-old reported of the 14-year-old.

"Sleeping?" I exclaimed, looking at the clock.

"Yeah, he said he needed 10 more minutes. That was about an hour ago." That sounded vaguely familiar.

"Have you heard from Phillip?" I continued my questioning through the ranks.

"He just got home," Andrew advised.

"Did he have fun at his sleepover?"

"I don't know," he responded, the shy pathetic voice tinted with irritation. (Boys don't ask boys such questions.)

"What about David?"

"Oh, he's climbing the wall right now."

"What?"

"You know, how we used to do that in the kitchen doorway," Andrew reassured me.

Breathing, I answered, "Yes, I remember. He showed me how he can do that the other day. Please tell him to stop. Who taught him that anyway?"

"Umm… It might have been me," Andrew admitted.

"No climbing the wall when I am not home!" I told Andrew to relay my message to his younger brother.

During the school year, my children don't even know that I have a job. I leave after they go to school and am home before they get off the bus. Summer is a different story. Two days a week, I leave early in the morning and arrive home by early afternoon.

Minus a few minor "tiffs" between siblings, the time spent together without direct adult supervision has been good for the children.

They have learned to help one another instead of calling for Mom.

"We couldn't get the television to work, so Phillip held the remote while I set the buttons," Robert informed me.

They have learned to take care of their needs (like eating) without relying on someone putting a plate in front of them.

"I am starving!" the 9-year-old said to me when I walked through the door. "I haven't eaten all day!"

"Why?"

"'Cause you didn't make my anything!"

I introduced him to peanut butter and jelly. Now, he has graduated to macaroni and cheese.

They deal with problems systematically: "I got David breakfast last time. Now, it's your turn."

There has been certain questionable behavior at times.

"Robert gave me sugar water," David informed me.

Glaring at my son, the 14-year-old explained.

"We were out of Kool-Aid. The child was thirsty," he defended his actions.

"It was really good," David smiled.

"The great, big brother came to the rescue!" Robert beamed, sticking out his chest, as I rolled my eyes.

"No more sugar water," I ruled.

I check in on the children periodically throughout the morning and they, of course, know how to get ahold of me.

"Hello, who is this?" a scratchy sounding voice asks me as I answer the phone at my desk.

"Who is this?" I ask in return.

"None of your business," the caller says.

Appalled, I respond, "I believe you have the wrong number."

I start to hang up when I hear laughter on the other end.

"I believe you have the wrong number," my son says, mimicking me.

"Hey Mom, you coming home soon?"

"Right now!" I yell into the phone.

Pranking mom at work will have to be added to the list of things not to do when home alone — right along with making sugar water and climbing the walls!

Oh, To Be 5 and In Love

Who would have thought that the first heartbreak I would have to contend with would be with my youngest child, a 5-year-old pre-schooler.

"Casanova" came home from school last year talking about Grace.

Being the caring, concerned, involved parent that I am (alright, neb-nosey mother), I got out the school picture and looked up this little girl my son had become so smitten over.

I had to admit, Grace was a cutie. Her long, black hair was over-shadowed only by her big, brown eyes and long, long lashes.

It wasn't long before David was calling her "My Gracie" and telling his brothers that he was going to marry her.

We all thought this was adorable. We soon realized how serious David was about this heartthrob.

"She's my Gracie," Robert taunted David one day. Being the young-est of four boys, David usually knows when he's being teased.

When it came to Grace, we soon found out he would tolerate no teasing. David hauled off and punched Robert square in the face!

Teachers started telling me how kind David was to Grace.

"If she's crying when she comes in the morning, he takes her hand and plays with her," one teacher told me.

"He sits next to her at lunch," another informed me.

"He's so gentle," still another said.

Tears would well up in my eyes every time they told me of his ac-tions. My greatest fear with this child was that he would be a raving lunatic at school after being power-bombed and karate-chopped by his older brothers from the time he could walk.

When that first year of preschool was over, David couldn't wait for the next school year to start in the fall so that he could see his

Gracie again.

When the first day of school finally arrived, David was beside himself with excitement. Little did he know, at 5-years-old, he was about to experience his first heartbreak.

Grace had changed over the summer.

She no longer cried when she came to school. She no longer needed a hand to hold. And, she wanted to play with the girls.

"Gracie gived-up on me," David informed. His sentiment was so cute, I wanted to smile, but the hurt in his eyes was heartbreaking.

"You'll always be friends," I told him, wondering what you tell a child at this age about love.

During a Mother's Day tea at preschool, we learned that Grace had appendicitis.

Her appendix had actually burst. She was recovering at home and would not be returning to preschool.

"We'll send her a get well card," I suggested to David.

"Maybe we could go see her?" he asked.

I called Grace's mother and arranged a time to visit.

We arrived at the house with a card and a china tea set.

After playing outside for a while, David and Grace sat down in the living room.

Talking with Grace's parents in the kitchen, we noticed how quiet the two had become. We peeked around the corner.

There they were, each with a teacup and saucer.

The two candles that came with the set were between them along with the napkin holder. Chocolate milk was in the teapot.

It was the cutest thing we had ever seen!

Grace was smiling sweetly, holding her teacup.

The smile from ear to ear on David's face told me that Casanova was back, at least for a moment.

I stared in amazement at this child. He made it look like I was raising the most polite, sophisticated young man in the world.

All sophistication was lost with one slip of the tongue.

When it was time to go, David took his cup and drank the rest of his "tea." Then, without blinking an eye, he picked up the saucer and licked it clean.

Man's Best Friend Captures Hearts of the Whole Family

When we moved into our house nine years ago, my husband insisted on getting a dog. We bought a yellow Labrador Retriever puppy from a farm a few miles away. I can still remember her sweet, shy demeanor as she laid next to her mother. We picked her up and she easily snuggled into our arms.

The children named her Laverne. My husband and I never knew how they came up with the name, but from the day we walked through the door with this puppy, Laverne was a member of our family.

As a pup, she was feisty. I recall one day when she saw the children at the end of the yard and came barreling toward them. She ran Phillip over, flipping him head over heels in her excitement.

We thought we lost her once. She was gone for two weeks. One day, there she was sitting on the back porch with a very guilty look on her face.

Two months later, we knew why. She had puppies.

We learned that the father was a golden retriever. The two had spent the two weeks together, sharing his dog house. Laverne, it seems, had fallen in love.

That's the kind of dog she was, loyal and faithful and true.

As much as she loved the golden retriever, however, she loved my husband more. They say a dog has one master. With Laverne, that was very true. That dog thought my husband hung the moon.

He played ball with her incessantly — that was part of the attraction. He talked to her with a sappy, lovey voice. She liked that too.

The clincher was when he started letting her sleep in the bed. (That was also the clincher for me!) In the evenings, while I put the children to bed, I would hear him call her. By the time I came to bed, Laverne would be comfortably sleeping in my spot.

"Get down!" I would demand. She would look to her master for instruction.

In the mornings, I would get up at 7 a.m. to get the children off to school. Laverne was up on the bed by 7:02.

There were days when she drove her master crazy. She followed him around the house everywhere he went.

While she loved my husband, she was wonderful with the children as well. She was the pillow for many small heads during cartoon shows. She was the horsey for rambunctious boys playing cowboys. She was the guard at the bus stop in the morning and the greeter in the afternoon.

As she got older, sleep became more important than fetching sticks. When we replaced our family room furniture, we saved the old love seat for Laverne. That was her couch.

Two years ago, we gave our son, Andrew, a dog for Christmas. It was a stray a friend had found living under her deck. The vet said the pup was about 4 months old when we rescued it, and he couldn't even venture a guess as to breed. Andrew called her Charlie.

Until now, Andrew was never really the master of his dog. He fed and watered her, but Laverne was Charlie's master.

Actually, she wasn't her master, she was her mother. That purebred, golden lab took that scroungy mutt under her wing and taught her the ways of the world.

The pup, in return, breathed new life into the old dog. She got up off her love seat and began running and playing again. The two were inseparable.

So, the day Laverne was hit by a car, Charlie wouldn't leave her.

"Your dog has been hit by a car," a neighbor called to tell us. "The little black dog won't leave her side."

Charlie wouldn't leave her side when we buried her in the woods. Long after we had said our goodbyes Charlie sat by the freshly dug dirt. She wouldn't eat or drink for days.

A few nights later, she sat at the end of the driveway and barked at the moon. If only the moon could cure a broken heart.

Our family is brokenhearted too. It's funny the things you miss the most.

Every time I pull into the driveway, I find myself looking for a wagging, yellow tail to come bounding out of the flower bed.

I hated it when Laverne was in my flower beds.

I'd love to see her there now.

Taking Stock in Lunch Trades

Every day, my fifth-grader comes home from school jingling two quarters around in this pocket. The quarters come from my son's friend, Alex, who pays him 50 cents each day for his juice.

When I learned this, I was horrified.

I pack 20 lunches a week. Therefore, the juice I purchase for the lunches is of the cheapest variety. There is absolutely no fruit content in this juice. It is merely colored sugar water.

"He could buy orange juice at school for 30 cents!" I told my son.

"He likes my juice," Phillip responded.

"What do you drink?" I asked.

"I get a drink from the water fountain," he said with a laugh, clearly valuing the two quarters more than the juice.

My discovery of this juice exchange prompted a dinner-long conversation on the profitability of lunch packing.

I believe stockbrokers on Wall Street could learn lessons in commodity trading and investment strategies from adolescents in the school lunchroom.

"You don't get anything for a sandwich," Robert informed me.

"Oh yes you can," Phillip chimed in. "When I bring egg salad, Katie will trade me for her kiwi."

While I pondered the exchange of passionfruit and eggs, the boys moved on to chips.

"Cheese curls are the best," Phillip informed me.

Variously flavored potato chips and Doritos are also hot items.

Pretzels are a bust.

Sometimes, the exchange can be quite equal: a bag of cheese curls for a bag of Doritos. Other times, the rationale behind the barter is understood only by the barterers.

"If I have cheese puffs and good cookies, Jen will trade me for her Lunchables pizza," Phillip beamed, proud of his brokering abilities.

"I can get $1.25 to $2 for kettle corn," Robert said, one-upping his brother.

Andrew had been conspicuously quiet during this dinner conversation. He is still in grade school. It seems the lunch brokering phenomenon begins in middle school.

"Sometimes I ask if anybody wants my apples," he said, somewhat confused by the entire conversation.

To this, of course, I frowned.

"Oh, you can get 25 cents to a cookie for an apple slice," Phillip declared happily.

"You sell your fruit?" I asked, looking disapprovingly at him. Then a recent conversation with this child came to mind.

"You told me to give you a whole apple in your lunch," I said warily.

"Yeah," Phillip answered, ignoring my look of displeasure. "You get more for a whole apple."

Apparently, lunch brokering is not relegated to just packers. Portions of a packed lunch can also be traded for certain school cafeteria lunch items.

Every Thursday, I learned, Phillip gives his entire lunch, except the sandwich, to an interested party in exchange for the garlic bread sticks sold in the cafeteria.

"You eat only bread products for lunch?" I asked, still reeling from the apple exchange.

I started thinking of the well-balanced lunches I pack half asleep, early, every morning.

"Why do I waste my time?" I asked myself aloud.

The boys weren't listening. They were deep into a discussion over the ultimate of lunchroom trades: dessert.

It seems, if you are willing to fork over your precious sugar-laden sweets, you can have just about anything in anyone else's lunch.

If the dessert is chocolate and creamy, the world is your oyster.

"If I have Oreos, I can get anything I want," Phillip said with a sly, confident look.

Robert nodded his head in agreement.

"Sometimes Justin gives me his Ho-Ho," Andrew said innocently.

"For what?" Phillip asked.

"Nothing," Andrew said, as he shrugged his shoulders. "He just gives it to me."

Robert and Phillip fell silent. A Ho-Ho for nothing.

Now that's a lunch broker's windfall!

The Christmas Pageant Miracle

Christmas is a celebration of the miraculous birth of Jesus to the virgin mother Mary. The re-enactment of that holy event is performed by churches across our country every year.

Children dress up as Mary and Joseph, shepherds and wise men memorize lines and stage directions to portray the Nativity.

After watching the dress rehearsal of the children's Christmas program at our church, I have determined that the miracle of Christmas did not end with the birth of the Holy Child. That miracle lives on every year, at every church that undertakes the task of a Christmas program.

It is truly a miracle that the show ever goes on.

I began to realize the magnitude of the miracle of the children's Christmas program when our youth minister called all the children onto the stage during dress rehearsal to run through their songs. (I believe leaders inclined to conquer the Christmas program have a special anointing from God. They have been given the gift of un-quenchable enthusiasm and a certain obliviousness to chaos.)

As the children stood on the stage, the leader wanted to re-arrange them.

"Everybody scoot down," he told them.

They all stared blankly at him.

"Scoot down," he repeated calmly.

Still no response registered in these young minds.

With the same patience and enthusiasm as when he asked the first time, this saint began calling each child by name.

"Eric, scoot down please," he began. Eric scooted.

"Melissa, scoot down," he asked the next child. Melissa scooted.

And so he continued down the line of children until they had all scooted to their proper position.

They began to sing.

I was impressed that every child seemed to know the words. The challenge was that not every child wanted to sing the words.

The boys in the back row began pushing one another. Those who weren't pushing looked tortured.

A little girl in the front row twirled her hair. One boy was more interested in bouncing than singing. A cute, chubby boy with big cheeks was making googly eyes at this neighbor.

The little cow stretched out his arms and yawned, then proceeded to pick his nose. An angel stood with her arms folded firmly in front of her with a not-so-angelic frown.

A mother and her young daughter sang a duet. The child forgot when to sing her lines.

As the performers for the Nativity filed in, the cows and donkey wandered aimlessly. Joseph hadn't made it to the dress rehearsal and the wise men stood in front of the shepherds.

"The show is tomorrow," I leaned over and whispered to a mother sitting next to me. "How is he going to pull this off?"

She shrugged and shook her head. Neither one of us could imagine.

At the end of the rehearsal, the leader, still enthusiastic said, "Great dress rehearsal! We are ready for tomorrow!"

I didn't think they would be ready for next year's Christmas program, let alone tomorrow!

But the leader knew something that I didn't fully understand. He knew the miracle of Christmas was not confined to the baby in the manger.

I witnessed that Christmas miracle the next evening, when those children walked onto that stage.

The boys in the back row stood still, sang loud and smiled.

The hair twirler in the front never touched her head. The bouncer still bounced, but he sang too. The cute, chubby boy with the big cheeks sang with all his might.

The cow didn't yawn and his fingers never touched his nose. The little angel looked absolutely angelic.

The mother and daughter duet made everyone cry, and the Nativity performers acted to perfection.

Those who came to the program were truly blessed. But those who attended the dress rehearsal witnessed a miracle!

Grandma's Got Baby-Sitting Job Sewed Up

My husband and I were planning a trip together. Just the two of us — no kids. (Yes!)

As excited as I was for our trip, the details that needed to be covered in our absence seemed overwhelming. Not the least of which was WHO would watch the children.

So, I called my mom. When you have four children — all boys — this is a huge question to ask of anyone.

I wasn't sure if Mom would say yes. For some reason, she did. (There must be some unwritten law that dictates Grandma must say yes. I don't understand it just yet, but I suspect my future holds the answer.)

It was a great relief knowing that my mother would be managing the household while I was gone. I turned my focus toward trip preparations.

My relief was short-lived. Conviction set in. As much as I tried to minimize the rigors of this obligation, I knew this was too much for mom.

In the middle of the night, I sat straight up in bed with a plan: Aunt Linda!

Actually, Aunt Linda is not my aunt, she is my great-aunt, which makes her my children's great-great-aunt.

"I am leaving town and my mom is coming to stay with the boys," I explained warily on the phone. "Will you come and stay with my mom?"

Miracle upon miracle, she said yes. In fact, and I quote, she said, "I would love to." Which is why I have decreed that henceforth this woman shall be called St. Great-Great-Aunt Linda.

My conviction was gone. The boys would have a ball with grandma and their great-great-aunt. Relief washed over me again — until worry set in.

It is difficult to leave your children. Even with the best-laid plans "things" can happen. And I can corner the market thinking about all those "things."

To relieve my worry, I wrote notes to Mom and Aunt Linda.

I had the children's morning schedule written out, including lunch packing. I made day-by-day notes on who was going where, when and with whom. I cooked several meals in bulk and placed them in the refrigerator, for which I made notes.

When I started making notes to explain notes, I knew I had gone off the deep end of worry.

As it turned out, I had nothing to worry about.

The boys had a fine time with Grandma and Aunt Linda. In between giving the technically challenged ladies repeated television remote control lessons (they never did figure out how to get to the channel they wanted) there were marathon Go Fish and Old Maid card games.

As I talked with the kids over the phone, I found myself a little upset at their lack of concern about my absence.

When I arrived home, I found a seven-page note from my mother detailing the events of her stay. (My note-writing was inherited.)

On the back of page 4, right after she apologized for the third time for anything that may be wrong with the television, she writes:

"Oh, before I forget, I sewed up the boys' night covers. Robert's had a hole in the corner with the stuffing coming out. … Stuffing was coming out of a corner of Phillip's blanket also. … I took the whole afternoon on Saturday and sewed up David's blanket. One whole side was open…" (Phillip had confessed trying to crawl through the hole.)

"I couldn't find one pair of scissors while sewing up David's blanket and discovered I had sewed them inside the blanket. … It's a good thing there was another hole along the other side of the blanket. That's how I retrieved the scissors."

She concludes, "There are NO scissors that I know of in David's blanket."

I worried about leaving my children with their grandmother and great-great-aunt.

With all my worrying, I never once thought to worry that my son could be knocked out by scissors sewn inside his blanket.

Driving with Son is a Rough Road

"Watch out for the ditch. The ditch. The ditch!"

These were my first words of advice for my 15 ½-year-old as he sat behind the wheel of the car.

He had received his driving permit the day before, and for the first time in years, was eager to go on any errand.

We were backing out of the driveway to go to the library when I found myself clutching the dashboard, gripped in fear, bracing for the plummet into the neighbors' drainage ditch.

Robert thought I was overreacting.

"I see the ditch mom," he said calmly.

I smiled faintly, trying to feign confidence in my child. "OK," I said, weak and white knuckled.

After several days of "adventures," I informed my husband one evening, "I don't think I should ride with Robert anymore. My gasping, holding my heart, clutching the dashboard and grasping at the ceiling is hurting his self-confidence," I admitted.

"You're kidding me," he said casually. "We're having a great time in the car when he drives. He's a good driver!"

Personally, I would not call Robert a "good" driver — yet. I will agree that he has great potential.

He conscientiously adjusts the side and rear-view mirrors every time he gets behind the wheel. He straps on his seat belt and makes sure everyone riding with him is wearing theirs. When he turned off the radio before putting the car in drive, I knew this child was serious about safety.

If only we could get to the point where my life stops flashing in front of my eyes.

In the past month, my life has fast-forwarded, reversed speed and nearly come to a screeching halt with Robert as my designated driver.

Just driving down the road takes my breath away — and possibly an arm.

He hugs the side of the road too close, and I find myself leaning toward him in my seat, certain that a mailbox is going to land on my lap.

Negotiating turns can be a real heart-stopper.

Maintaining his affinity for ditches, Robert pulled out to go left on a busy road one afternoon and nearly introduced us to the ditch on the other side.

Turning right off our road one evening, he didn't turn the wheel enough and went all the way across the double yellow line into the other lane. I have never been more thankful for cars that are not there.

"That was too fast!" I squawked when I regained my breath. (It has become a mantra that I now bellow out in my sleep.)

Then there are times when I contradict my own advice.

Pulling out of the video store, he negotiated the right hand turn a little too tight and nipped the curb. He took his foot off the gas after the first tire went over the curb. I looked out his window and saw a semi-truck barreling down upon us.

"Gun it!" I screamed.

And then there is the inevitable stop.

I would have to say, this is one of Robert's best beginning skills. He seems to have a pretty good feel for the brake. He does, however, tend to start the process a little too late.

"There's a red light up there," I informed him one morning on the way to school.

"I know mom," he replied in his ever calm voice.

"You need to slow down. Start braking! Hit the brakes!"

Though he has almost killed me several times, I feel sorry for the child. Truly, I would not want to learn to drive with me.

But there is light for both of us at the end of the road.

We were running an errand to the store, Robert in the driver's seat, me riding shotgun. As he went to turn the corner at the end of our road, I assumed my usual position, one hand on the dash, the other grasping the roof.

His negotiation was smooth and precise: textbook perfect.

"Nice! Very nice!" I said, beaming proudly at him.

He turned his head and smiled back, proud of himself.

It was a wonderful moment that nearly ended with us hitting a mailbox.

It's Fun to Receive, but Nothing Beats Giving

It was 6:20 a.m. and I could hear the pitter-patter of little feet.

The bedroom door opened and a child stood in the doorway, breathing.

The door closed and the feet pitter-pattered away.

It was Saturday and I was hoping to sleep in. But every so often I would hear the little feet, the door and the breathing. (I learned later that the child was checking to see if I was awake during commercial breaks.)

When the first commercial break after 8 a.m. arrived, 6-year-old David could wait no more.

"Mom, are you awake?" he whispered as he crawled into bed beside me. "Is it time to go get presents for everybody?"

"No," I whispered back groggily. "The store is not open yet."

The night before, the boys had wrapped their Christmas gifts to one another. Three would hurriedly wrap a gift while one was held at bay in another room. When everyone's gift had been wrapped, David began to cry.

"I didn't get to do anything!" he wailed. "They got to do it all!" The boys, meanwhile, would have been happy not to do any of it.

To heal his broken heart, I promised to take him to the store the next day where he could buy presents for everybody and wrap them all himself.

Technically, 6 a.m. was the next day and David was ready to shop. We were out the door by 9:30.

I let him sit in the front seat for the first time. He proudly strapped the seat belt around himself and showed me how he had strapped his Batman figurine in too. He chattered happily the whole way to the store.

"This is taking a million years," he said, after he had asked if we were almost there yet again.

As we arrived in the parking lot, he could barely contain himself. He bounded out of the car and headed for the store. A man held the door for him as David bounced and gyrated in, making strange noises.

"He's excited," I explained to the man.

"I guess so," he said with a smile.

David walked through the aisles with a shopping basket on his arm, carefully considering each item. This was a more serious matter than I had imagined.

He chose a sword for Phillip.

"I think Phillip already has a sword." I cringed at the thought of another long, lamp-breaking toy. David decided I was right and picked a jumbo Chutes and Ladders game. "I can't wait 'til he opens this!" he beamed.

I could not change his mind on his gift for his grandfather, however. He picked out a bright blue stocking with a snowman on it.

"Why don't we look for something else," I suggested.

"No," David said very adamantly. "He's going to love this."

When we found a doll named Jamie I thought the child would burst. "Jamie!" his eyes were as big as saucers. He did not have the words to express how much his cousin Jamie was going to love that doll.

"I can't wait until Christmas!" he said, beaming wistfully as he sat in the car on the way home, hugging his bag of presents closely to his chest.

I looked over at him. He wasn't excited thinking about all the gifts he was going to get this Christmas. He was thinking about his bag full of presents that he was giving.

He wrapped them all the moment we got home.

They look like a pile of mangled paper under the tree. Not one of them has a tag to show whom the gift is for.

But David knows what's in each one. And when each member of our family receives their crumpled, creased, taped-up package, they'll know exactly where it's from — David's heart.

Favorite in a Foxhole

We were watching an old war movie when one of life's all-important questions came up: Which one of my children would I want to be with in a foxhole?

I had never considered the thought before. And after our discussion, I don't ever want to consider it again!

Bottom line: If I'm ever in a foxhole with any of my children, I'm in trouble.

My oldest son, Robert, 21, is a very laid back, I'll-get-there-when-I-get-there kind of child. He refused to go to college (It was not his "gig"), lives on his own, "scored" a primo apartment this year, and helps run a bakery in town. He loves to bake.

He announced at Easter dinner that he is considering throwing out his cell phone and just working, reading and writing for the next year. We never quite know what he's going to say next.

If I were in a foxhole with Robert, we would be crouched in the corner "vegging out."

"Yo, Mom," he would say. "Let's just chill here and wait this thing out."

One of his brothers added that if the enemy found us hiding in the foxhole, Robert would flash them the peace sign and say, "Sup, Dude?"

"And no one would shoot him," Phillip said, envisioning such an encounter. "He'd be telling jokes and playing poker with the enemy by nightfall."

Phillip, 18, on the other hand, is the exact opposite of his older brother. He knew exactly where he wanted to go to college since the beginning of his sophomore year, has a timeline of what he hopes to accomplish and when, and every minute planned out in between.

If I were in a foxhole with Phillip, he would be in my face, intensity in his eyes, drawing strategic pictures in the mud on the wall. There would be no time for questions or reiteration.

"Move! Move! Move!" he would yell, running out of the hole, guns strapped to both sides, spraying bullets in all directions.

"Like Butch Cassidy and the Sundance Kid," I said dryly, thinking about their demise.

"No," Phillip insisted. "I would kill everyone."

Andrew, 16, would probably be my best bet. Andrew is as cool as a cucumber. Once as a new driver, he was cruising down the freeway when a tire blew. While I was startled and screaming, he calmly steered the car to the side of the road, parked and waited for me to calm down and call the motor club.

Andrew would be in the foxhole surveying the situation, planning an attack or retreat, whichever he felt would provide the best outcome with absolutely no consideration regarding the cause or purpose of the battle. He would be methodical, patient and precise when issuing directions.

The problem with Andrew is, should the going get tough, he would use me as a body shield against the enemy and put me right out there in front of him to block the bullets.

When this was brought up in our discussion, Andrew replied, "Well, you have to protect yourself."

David, 11, would be the sweetest foxhole companion, With the two of us in a foxhole, David would be asking, "Are you OK, Mom? Can I get you anything, Mom? Do you want my helmet, Mom?"

But with all his concern for me, when the time came to defeat the enemy, David would go running out of the foxhole, ready to protect himself and his mother, but as soon as his feet touched the ground, he would inevitably stop in his tracks, grasping himself up and down in utter, total confusion and ask, "Where's my gun? Did I leave it in the foxhole? Do you have my gun, Mom? Where did I put my gun?"

Needless to say, the entire foxhole scenario gave me nightmares for a week. My prospects were dim — captured by the enemy while "chilling," completely obliterated in a blitzkrieg, shot in the front being used as a shield or shot in the back on a search and find mission.

Leave it to the 11-year-old to brighten the moment. "You're too old to be in a foxhole anyway, Mom."

Mother of the Year

I have officially become one of "those" moms.

I am the mom that other moms whisper about in hushed circles. I forget things I should remember. I don't care about things that other moms find immensely important.

I used to be a "mother-of-the-year" kind of mom: classroom volunteer, committee chairperson, den mother. I was on top of every activity my kids were involved in.

Now, with two children graduated and one graduating this year, my youngest child, David, a sixth-grader, has a much more laid back, let's-not-sweat-the-small-stuff, mothering experience.

While this can be a good characteristic for a type A mom, I realized at the beginning of this school year that I needed to "sweat" some stuff.

David had forgotten his lunch money. I didn't want him to panic at lunch time, so I emailed his teacher, Mrs. Cappuzzello, informing her that he had forgotten his money and for him to tell the cafeteria that we will pay tomorrow.

It was a very "mother-of-the-year" thing to do, except Mrs. Cappuzzello is not his teacher this year.

She emailed me back, said it was all taken care of and he was fine. It wasn't until Open House when I started to walk in her room to look at David's seat and class work when my son informed me Mrs. Cappuzzello was not one of his teachers.

"But I emailed you..." I stammered, looking at her.

"And I took care of it. It was fine!" Mrs. Cappuzzello said light-heartedly.

We laughed hysterically at the realization of what I had done.

My laissez-faire mothering went unnoticed after the Open House incident, until parent-teacher conferences.

David had received a B and he was highly disturbed. (I have two children who were thrilled with B's and two that find them completely unacceptable.)

I was scheduled to meet with all three of David's teachers in a group session. Walking into the school, I realized that two of David's sixth grade teachers have taught all of my children. For Mrs. Wattenbarger and Mrs. Ferrand, this would be my fourth parent-teacher conference.

David's homeroom teacher, Mrs. Guarnieri, is new to the district this year. David is the only one of my children she will ever teach. I am quite certain she is thanking her lucky stars for that!

The conference started like a group of old friends chatting. I recapped what all the older boys were doing now, asked Mrs. Wattenbarger about her son and laughed over the antics of Mrs. Ferrand's grandchildren.

Moving on to discuss David, Mrs. Wattenbarger said he is a lovely child, she really enjoys having him in class. Mrs. Ferrand said he is a joy, very helpful and friendly. He had missed an assignment, thus the "B."

When I turned to talk with Mrs. Guarnieri, she had a stern look on her face.

"Well, actually..." she spoke rather slowly. "I am having a bit of trouble with David."

"Oh?" I said, losing the casual, carefree tone of the meeting.

"I have David first and last periods," Mrs. Guarnieri explained. "During first period, he won't sit still, he's bouncing around in his seat, and he's uncontrollably hyper."

"How odd," I responded. Mrs. Ferrand and Mrs. Wattenbarger nodded, adding that they don't have any trouble with David in this manner.

"By last period, he's droopy, barely pays attention and is ready to fall asleep," Mrs. Guarnieri continued.

We all stared at her, puzzled.

"So I asked him if he had trouble sleeping at night, or took medication or ate sugary cereal in the morning," Mrs. Guarnieri said, as I shook my head on all counts. "He said he didn't," Mrs. Guarnieri agreed with my assessment, then stared me in the eyes. "But he said he likes to drink coffee in the morning."

My gasp sucked the air right out of the room.

"Oh dear," I whispered, putting my head down. "Yes, David drinks coffee in the morning." (We both prepare a cup to take in the car and we have pleasant coffee talk on the way to school.)

I could hear the gavel in Mrs. Guarnieri's head, "Guilty as charged!" Meanwhile, Mrs. Wattenbarger and Mrs. Ferrand burst into uproarious laughter.

"Well, I never!" Mrs. Wattenbarger howled.

"In all my years, I haven't heard that one!" Mrs. Ferrand said, bursting at the seams.

Unamused, Mrs. Guarnieri continued, "I told him perhaps he should try decaffeinated coffee."

My head still down, I responded, "That wouldn't help. He puts a ton of sugar in it."

"So he's having a caffeine-sugar crash last period!" Mrs. Ferrand wailed, putting her hand over her mouth in an attempt to control her laughter.

"That's a classic!" Mrs. Wattenbarger said pounding the table, nearly in tears.

I vaguely remember wondering if David's souped-up coffee was affecting him. Now I knew.

"I am so sorry. It won't happen again," I promised Mrs. Guarnieri with a most earnest mother-of-the-year apology.

David's Time for "The Talk"

My fifth-grader came home from school one afternoon and announced, "We had 'The Talk' today, Mom."

"The Talk?" I feigned confusion, knowing full well what he meant.

He leaned toward me and lowered his voice like he was telling a secret. "The *sex* talk," he whispered.

"Ooohh," I whispered back. "Did you learn anything?"

"Not really," he said, his shyness over the topic gone and his 11-year-old preteen confidence coming back. "Timmy said he could have taught the class."

"Really?" I responded, stifling a laugh.

"Yeah, he said he knew all about this stuff already," David said. "And Michael said he was sick of hearing about hormones, hormones, hormones!"

"Well, what did you think?" I asked.

"I think the doctor was wrong," David said, very matter-of-factly.

"Wrong?" I asked, amazed at the child's audacity. As the youngest of four boys, David knows way too much for his age. (Or at least he thinks he knows!)

"Yeah, the doctor said that boys go through puberty between 12 and 15, but I'm already in puberty."

I knew what was coming next. He had shared this tidbit of information with me before.

David cocked his head, nodded and reminded me, "I have a hair." (emphasis on "a")

"Yes, the hair," I nodded, practically bursting at the seams.

David had been riding in the car with his friend Vince, when Vince mentioned to David that he thought David's voice sounded deeper.

David informed Vince that he did indeed have a hair "down there," and the two of them determined that David was going through puberty. David shared this information with his brothers, who responded with absolutely no restraint in their laughter.

I, on the other hand, was mortified that Vince's mother heard this conversation. Vince is the oldest boy in his family, and I was quite certain that his two older sisters had never had such conversations.

In talking with Vince's mom, she had taken the whole thing in stride. I jokingly reminded her of the time it was "Lunch with a Parent" day at school and I witnessed Vince eat his entire serving of mashed potatoes and gravy by sucking it up through a straw. We decided we were even.

"So, did the doctor talk about anything else?" I asked David, trying to move on from the hair.

"Yeah," David nodded, his voice returning to a whisper. "STD's."

I was a little taken aback by this. "Really?" I asked, trying to hide my shock. "What did he say?"

"Well, they're gross and bad," David shared, his confidence coming back a bit on the subject.

"Yes...yes..." I muttered, trying to figure out what to ask next. I know it's important to discuss these things, but I just wasn't sure how far to go into detail with him.

David's next words solved my dilemma.

"Yeah," the 11-year-old said, casually leaning up against the kitchen counter, an air of know-it-all about him. "The doctor told us about STD's, like clams and AIDS."

"*Clams* and AIDS?" I asked.

"Yep," David nodded, proud of his new-found knowledge. "Can I go play?"

"Absolutely," I smiled.

The "clams" and AIDS talk could wait until another day.

Feeling the Big Chill

Alexis leaned across the car to talk to me out the passenger window as I stood in the driveway.

"Phillip and I are going to go golfing," she said, with her pretty, 16-year-old smile.

"That will be fun," I smiled back, trying to sound genuinely excited. And I was excited for them. Being young and carefree, enjoying every minute of summer is a great time in life. But I couldn't ignore the cold chill I felt down the back of my neck.

I had felt that chill before, the first time I met my oldest son's first girlfriend. He had his arm around her and they were talking and laughing casually, but very close. I truly struggled with whether to hug her or pull his arm out from around her.

That chill is a very strange feeling, a stirring combination of mama bear, the panic you feel when you've lost something and the warm fuzzies. The mix of emotions is absolutely jarring.

I prefer the pre-teenage days when "liking someone" meant you absolutely did not talk to them.

Phillip was called on the carpet one day in fourth grade when one of his friends informed me that not only did he like a certain girl, he talked to her all the time. After intense questioning, he assured me they weren't "going out" they were "just friends." (The "going out" always cracks me up with elementary kids.)

Then there was the time in ninth grade when Phillip asked a girl to the winter homecoming dance.

A few weeks before the date, he popped into the kitchen one evening and asked, "Mom, can we pick up Kristin when we go to the basketball game tonight? And then can she come here for a little while after the game?"

In spite of a slight chill, I said yes.

On the way to Kristin's house I was coaching Phillip. "Now, if her mother or father come to the door, make sure you look them straight in the eye when you say hello and have a good, firm handshake. Speak coherently, don't mumble and smile a lot."

Rolling his eyes, Phillip nodded to my instructions.

I was nervously watching as he ascended the steps to her house. (I was nervous; he was not.) I watched as he knocked on the door, talked briefly to someone, shook hands, and then Kristin appeared.

They said a few words to each other on the porch and then...

The next thing I knew, they were both racing toward the car. Phillip nudged Kristin a little on the steps. He came barreling up to the front passenger door, plastering his body against the glass. Quickly, he opened the door, hopped in the front seat and slammed the door shut, sitting there with a very smug smile.

Kristin stood outside the back door for a second, looking dejected, then opened the door and slumped into the seat.

I was nearly speechless (nearly — but not quite.)

"F!" I yelled at Phillip. "You get an 'F' on how to treat a young lady! That was AWFUL! You didn't walk her to the car! You didn't open the door for her! And you're sitting up here and she's in the back seat all by herself!"

"I am very sorry, Kristin," I said, looking at her sympathetically.

"Really, it's OK," she said. "We both called shotgun."

Our Labor Day Invasion

When my oldest son, Robert, moved to an apartment in Columbus, I missed him terribly. I made a promise to myself not to overstep boundaries by over-mothering.

He was very thankful the first time we visited and I brought food saving containers for him, all filled with various delicacies from home. While he devoured a huge plate of spaghetti and meatballs, he didn't mind a bit that I hung the curtains I had given him for his living room. I found them rolled up in a bag in a corner of the apartment.

I learned quickly that food was a perfect salve for my intermittent moments of over-mothering. (Actually, "intermittent" may not be exactly the correct word.)

There is not enough food in the world, however, for what our family has deemed "The Labor Day Invasion."

With the holiday approaching, I couldn't stand the thought of not spending it with Robert. I thought we'd make a weekend of it, visiting him in Columbus and then heading to Cincinnati to visit my brother and his family.

When weekend plans didn't work out, I determined a Sunday road trip to Columbus was the way to go. My sister-in-law, Nicole, said she and my nephew would meet us there.

Early Sunday morning, my parents called and decided they were game for a road trip as well.

We arrived in Columbus about 11:30. As we all filed out of our cars and I saw the shocked look on Robert's face, I realized I had committed a gargantuan overstep in the boundary department.

After a round of hugs, Robert was helping me take food, lawn chairs and a table out of the van.

"Mom," he hissed. "This is not cool! You cannot have a family picnic at my apartment!"

Realizing what I had done, I was speechless. I mumbled an apology and handed him the steaks I brought for a cookout, grabbed the wall hangings I bought for above his couch and headed inside.

Nicole and I hung the wall hangings while Grandma determined "straight" and "crooked" from her chair.

The boys were either playing video games or throwing a football from the living room to the kitchen, while Grandpa was busy outside, firing up the grill and setting up lawn chairs.

Robert roamed around, still in a stupor over his invasion.

We all sat down to eat under a tree by the sidewalk in front of the apartment — except for Robert who was standing, trying desperately to hide is face in his plate, when his roommate arrived home.

"You Hungry, Adam?" Grandpa asked.

He didn't have to be asked twice.

Adam grabbed a plate of food and sat down.

The guy living in the apartment next door walked by.

Robert's nose was so close to his plate it looked like he was vacuuming his food.

Adam introduced the neighbor and he, too, was invited to our picnic.

There we sat all afternoon, laughing and talking in the tiny green space in front of Robert's apartment.

Adam and Brian kept the conversation lively while Robert looked on, still silent.

As we visited, two other neighbors were busy moving out. They threw a lounge chair into the dumpster. A car came by, stopped, and the driver put the chair in his trunk.

The movers carried out a large piece of plywood.

"Ohhh!" Brian moaned. "You're getting rid of the beer pong table?"

The neighbors nodded.

Grandpa, a very upstanding man, looked indignant. We all braced for a lecture.

"You're throwing that away?" He asked. "That's a good piece of plywood!"

Before we knew it, those neighbors had joined our picnic as well.

All too soon, it was time for Robert to go to work. But the rest of the family wasn't done picnicking yet. So, I left everyone sitting outside talking with the neighbors at the apartment and drove Robert to the restaurant where he works, apologizing profusely the entire way.

As he got out of the car, I quipped, "Promise we won't be there when you get home!"

It garnered only a faint smile from Robert and a slight look of panic that we may, indeed, all still be sitting under the tree when he arrived home.

He didn't have to worry, however. When we finally packed up and said our goodbyes to the neighborhood, we decided that we were now hungry again.

So, we headed downtown to the restaurant with our favorite chef.

As the eight of us walked in and approached his station, the smile that had been missing all day came across Robert's face.

"You just couldn't stay away, could you?" he said, ruffling his cousin's hair.

"Sorry?" I said, weakly.

But this time, he knew that I really wasn't.

For one slight, fraction of a moment, I sensed a tinge of gratitude for our invasion.

Birthday Suit Surprise

It was my birthday and my wonderful husband surprised me with a trip to Florida.

He was coming in from Houston, meeting me at the airport in Florida, and we were driving down through the Keys to spend several days in Key West.

I, of course, was very happy with this unexpected birthday surprise. When I woke up the morning I was to leave and found the air had a crisp, fall feel to it, I was even more thrilled with the thought of leaving town.

I arrived at the airport on a tight time frame. I had checked in online, so I wasn't too worried about catching my plane, but I knew I didn't have a lot of time to spare.

Hurriedly, I pulled my carry-on bag out of the trunk and briskly walked through the parking lot. I had decided to dress for Florida weather, so I was wearing a short, white skirt and a silky black tank top with a black jacket, out of necessity. I couldn't wait to take off the jacket when I landed in the Sunshine State. But as I was walking through the parking lot, I was glad I had the jacket and was rather wishing I had chosen pants as the cool wind blew up through my skirt.

I was in an absolutely euphoric mood, feeling trendy about leaving town and anticipating a fun-filled weekend in one of the most carefree places on earth!

I had almost reached the indoor moving sidewalk when a man exited the walkway coming toward me. He must have noticed my smile and my less-than-warm clothing as he commented, "Going someplace warm, I hope?"

Feeling smug and even a little cocky, I replied in my smoothest voice, "Absolutely!" And I cocked my head a little higher, pleased with having been noticed.

By the time I had reached the walking sidewalk, I was on a full-blown ego trip.

When my phone rang and I had to handle a business call, the moment was complete. I was a jet-set traveler, escaping the daily grind for a long weekend adventure.

Slightly concerned about catching the flight, I picked up my pace. As I hurried along, I came up behind an older woman standing still on the walk with her bags on either side of her.

Hearing me coming up behind her, she grabbed her bags and took a few steps forward. In my cocky state of mind, I rolled my eyes at her from behind. Did she really think she was going to keep up pace with me?

She stopped and moved to one side of the walk. "Thank you," I smiled at her, a little condescending, I'm sure.

And I breezed on by.

A few steps later I heard, "Honey, do you know your rear end is hanging out?"

I almost ignored the voice behind me and kept on going, but then my ego-riddled brain processed the words.

I stopped and turned around. "Excuse me?" I asked.

"Your rear end is hanging out of your skirt," she informed me in a way that only someone who has been around this world a long time and has reached the point where nothing could surprise.

I reached my hand back to the bottom of my skirt with a confused look.

"No," the older woman informed me. "Higher."

Moving my hand up the back seam there it was, a hole the size of the Florida panhandle. The seam was completely ripped out.

My mouth dropped open, all the cocky ego attitude was gone with the wind — that had been blowing through my skirt!

"Oh, my!" I exclaimed, with a look of total helplessness and desperation.

Just then a twenty-something couple came running up.

"We were trying to catch up with you to tell you!" the girl said, a bit winded from her run.

Meanwhile, my hand was fixed on my behind.

"Take your jacket off and wrap it around your waist," the girl suggested.

"Yes!" I agreed and quickly took off my jacket. Wrapping it around my waist I looked at my ham-hock arms hanging loose with the tank covering nothing. "Oh no!" I lamented. "I can't walk around like this!"

"Well, it's better than the alternative!" the twenty-something guy said with a look of disgust. (I believe my hanging rear left a scar on his young brain!) The older woman nodded her head in agreement. The matter was not up for discussion. The jacket stayed covering my behind.

Completely humbled, my "trendiness" lost, I thanked my hind-end safeguards profusely and hurried into the security line, wondering what I was going to say to the TSA agents if they asked me to remove my jacket.

Doggone It, Who's Missing?

I was driving home from work when I pulled up behind my neighbor, Jen, driving very slowly down the road, looking intently in every direction.

"Watchadoin'?" I asked her as I pulled up along side her mini-van.

"Lexi is missing," Jen responded, completely exasperated.

Lexi is the Sloan family's pet dog, one of two dogs and a cat that inhabit the home along with Jen and John's four sons, all under the age of 12. It is a busy household every minute of the day.

"Kenny came over today and asked where Lexi was," Jen continued to explain. "I didn't even know she was gone! One of the kids must have left the gate open in the back yard."

Adding to the busyness of the Sloan household is Kenny, a middle-aged man, mentally challenged, with no family of his own. He has adopted the Sloan family and on any given day, can be found doing chores, helping with the kids, mowing the grass and, luckily, noticing missing pets.

A missing dog is the last thing Jen needs to add to her list of things to do today — or apparently yesterday or the day before.

"I'll get David out looking for her," I told Jen.

"Thanks!" she smiled with a heavy sigh and we both drove off.

It was two days later before I talked with Jen again.

"Did you find your dog?" I asked as I popped in on her one afternoon.

Kenny, who was sweeping the kitchen floor, broke out into uproarious laughter.

Jen put her head down in shame and replied, "Yes, she's back home."

It seems that after Kenny had discovered Lexi missing and Jen went searching for her, John came home from work that evening and called the police station.

They, indeed, had a report of a dog that had been found. They gave him the name and number of the person who reported it.

"It was right around the corner, so I just went to the house," John explained. When he got there the woman said she had found a dog but she just couldn't take care of it anymore so she took it to the pound.

"Couldn't take care of it anymore?" John replied kindly. "It was just this afternoon."

The woman told him she had had the dog for three days.

"Well, it can't be my dog," John scoffed. "Lexi's just been missing for a couple of hours."

"I have pictures," the woman told him. "I made fliers."

(To get the full effect, one needs to see John's face when he tells this part of the story. But just imagine complete, total shock and humiliation.)

"She brought out her camera," John stumbles on his words. "And showed me the pictures... (there is a long pause) 'Damn!' I said. That's my dog!"

Yes, Lexi had been missing for three days and if it hadn't been for Kenny, Lexi would have spent her final days at the pound. (The dog has several health issues and was deemed unadoptable by the pound's standards.)

When Lexi returned home, the family rejoiced with hugs and kisses and cries that she was so missed.

Jen wonders why none of the boys noticed their precious pet was gone and worries that if she can go days without noticing a dog is missing in the chaos of the household, could she not notice one of the boys missing?

She would probably lay awake at night fretting over this possibility, except for the fact that she is completely exhausted by the time her head hits the pillow every evening.

Besides, she has Kenny to keep tabs on her brood.

Tall Tales From the Injured Reserve

When I received a call from the little league football coach, I knew it wasn't good.

"Gail, it's Rick. David hurt his knee and..."

I cut him off before he finished his sentence. "I'll be right there."

Pulling in to the practice field parking lot, I saw no fewer than 20 people crowded around the back of an SUV. Getting out of the car, I could hear the whimper of a child crying. The crowd parted to let me through. There was David, lying down, tears streaming down his face. His football pants had been cut open and the knee was iced and bandaged.

The coaches shared their versions of what had happened and advised, since it was his knee, that I take David to the emergency room and have it X-rayed.

David is my fourth son to play football. Miraculously, I had avoided any trips to the emergency room with the other three.

The experience taught me a few things.

First, I realized that I absolutely LOVE the sport of golf (which I strongly urged David to take up as we drove to the hospital).

The second thing I learned was that fishermen and their tall tales have nothing on little league football players. Those kids in helmets can spin a tale from goal post to goal post.

About an hour after we arrived at the hospital, my phone started ringing.

Calls from coaches, concerned parents and David's friends started flooding in. (Apparently news of David's injury had been posted on Facebook as well.)

As he left the hospital with a diagnosis of a deep knee sprain, I listened to all the messages.

"Gail, please call and tell me how David is. The boys said his knee swelled up to the size of a football!" a friend of mine had called. David's knee had very little swelling.

"I hope David's knee is OK," one unidentified friend of his called. "His knee was completely black and blue!" There was a small, round bruise on my son's knee.

David wanted to call his friend Timmy, who had also left a message.

Timmy's mother answered. "How are you David?" she asked, with deep concern in her voice.

"Well," David said, very dramatically. "It's not broken, but it's fractured."

"Sprained," I corrected him.

"Oh, it's sprained. It's going to hurt for a while they said," David continued. "I also have a cyst on my knee, which is like an extra bone..."

"Give me the phone!" I yelled, amazed at his exaggeration about the mark on his knee from where the doctor said he must have hurt it before.

"And he has a twisted liver," I told Timmy's mom, who howled with laughter. Her older son had been injured a few years earlier and Timmy told all his friends that his brother was suffering from a twisted liver.

"How do they come up with this stuff?" Heather marveled.

The drama continued when David returned to practice a few days later.

His friend Matt came running up to me. "I'm so glad David's OK! That's just amazing since his kneecap moved over 3 inches!"

"It is amazing," I replied, laughing. "It's absolutely amazing!"

Defibrillators, Please!

It was two weeks before Easter and I was shopping at the local supermarket when I ran into one of my son's friends.

"Alex!" I smiled, giving him a hug. "I miss you!"

It's sad, when a child goes off to college, you not only lose him, but his friends too. (This is actually both good and bad!)

"I haven't talked to Phillip in over a week," I told Alex. "Have you talked to him lately?"

Alex, normally a very smooth, casual talker, started to stutter.

"Oh... Oh!" He stammered. "Well, I...ahhhh...haven't talked to him all that recently... I'm sure he's just fine...Yes, I'm sure everything is alright with him..."

My mouth dropped to the grocery store floor. "You are freaking me out, Alex," I said. "Is something going on with Phil?"

Alex's stammering turned into Tourette's. He scrunched his chin into his neck and shook his head vigorously from side to side, all the while trying to maintain control of his voice.

"Nooo..." he insisted. "I'm sure everything is good with Phil."

I was in shock. I stared the child down. "I don't believe you, Alex," I informed him. "Whatever is going on, is it going to give me a heart attack?" I asked him.

Alex was still in Tourette's mode but became increasingly interested in the can of soup he was holding as he answered, "No... I hope not."

"Well, you have just given me one!" I said to the boy.

Alex stopped fidgeting and looked me in the eye, "I'm sure you will be hearing from him very soon..." Heart attack number two right there.

Then he added, "Don't tell Phil you saw me." Defibrillators, please!

Driving home, I recounted Phil's school experiences: three weeks after we dropped him off in Chicago his freshman year, he was mugged at gunpoint; sophomore year, he tripped while running on the sidewalk on his way to the convenient store and broke his collar bone; going into his junior year he was homeless for a couple of weeks before his apartment was available. For ALL these things, I received a phone call from the child.

"Dear God," I prayed, "What could possibly be wrong?"

At home, I shared my odd encounter with Alex with my husband. "This is bad," I told him. "What do you think could be going on with Phil?"

"Well," Bill replied. "He's either dropped out of school or gotten a girl pregnant." (I don't know if he was trying to make me feel better or preparing me for the absolute worst, but the consensus of everyone with whom I have shared this story is that this was a really bad answer!)

There was only one way to get my heart beating normally again. I called Phillip.

He answered the phone in his normal, cheery manner, "Hi Mom!"

"Hi Phillip!" I feigned delight. "How's it going?"

He talked about one of his classes he was writing a paper for and a bunch of other stuff I didn't pay attention to because I was too busy listening to the tone in his voice, trying to detect some hint of trouble or deceit.

"What else is new?" I asked.

He yammered on some more about a bunch of stuff he was working on outside of school.

"Anything else new?" I continued my query. I couldn't detect one ounce of oddness or hesitation on his part, and certainly not the slightest hint of Tourette's!

Finally, I couldn't take it anymore. Even though I knew I was breaking my promise, I said, "I saw Alex today." I paused, waiting to see if this caused a reaction. Nothing.

Exasperated, I said, "He went totally deer-in-the-headlights when I asked about you. What is going on?"

I did notice a hint of hesitation with Phillip this time. "Oh, you know Alex," he said. "He's just crazy weird."

"Are you sure nothing is going on?" I insisted. "You didn't drop out of school? Get a girl pregnant?"

Phillip laughed. "No, Mom. I tell Alex stuff. We were talking the other day. Who knows what he's thinking!"

"Ok," I said, still a little leery but very relieved.

A week later, I was standing in the kitchen cutting up some vegetables when a figure came up behind me.

It was Phillip on a surprise visit home from school for Easter!

Alex had picked him up from the Megabus in Cleveland.

Hanging In Her 50s

In light of recent revelations about being in my 40s — the free-spirited feeling, the joy of being comfortable with yourself and not worrying what others think — a friend of mine enlightened me about the next decade.

Apparently, the free-spirited, no-worry attitude of the 40s becomes a valuable coping mechanism in your 50s.

Susan is a very fit, active woman. She's trendy and fun and is often mistaken for being much younger than her age, which is best described as two quarters plus. A couple of times a week we exercise by walking through the park.

We have found that our conversation tends to grow quiet when we walk up hills nowadays, and we seem to need to stop and use the restroom a lot more than we used to.

But on this walk, there was no quiet lull as I laughed both up and down the hills, and the restroom was not nearly close enough as she related her pee-your-pants funny tale.

"Do you notice your arms losing muscle?" Susan asked, the conversation starting off quite innocently.

"I guess, a little," I replied.

"Just wait," she smirked back. And with that, her story began.

It seems Susan and her husband, Karl, were boating with friends over the weekend. While the swimming and tubing were great fun, getting back in the boat was not.

"I couldn't pull myself up," she said with a hint of whine.

Bobbing up and down in the water, lifejacket hugging her neck, she grasped, pulled and straddled to get herself onto the boat.

At one point, with one leg up on the deck, she thought she had it. Her arms reached for a hold as she desperately tried to pull the rest of her body out of the water.

Just when she thought she would surely split in two, the water won the battle as it pulled her landlubber leg off the deck, taking the rest of her body with it.

"I thought I might have to sleep out there," she said, now in a full-blown pout.

Karl came to the rescue with helpful hands. Bobbing up and down behind her, they counted to three and he hoisted her buttocks upward as hard as he could. The effort proved to be a great success in getting her out of the water. Not so great for her dignity.

While the boatload of friends cheered at her emergence from the water, Susan lay splayed out on the deck like (her words) "a fish flapping around on dry land."

The life vest was up to her nose. One arm was under her, the other seemed to have acquired some sort of palsy from being in the water so long, and her legs were completely useless.

Once the cheering stopped and she was still lying on the deck, the boat load of friends asked if she was all right.

"I'm fine! Just give me a minute!" she said, praying that at least one limb would start to work soon.

Her limbs did, eventually, return to their useful state, but not before she vowed never to jump off a boat again more than a distance she could swim to land.

Back on shore, the group decided to celebrate their day's adventure with a drink. Jumping into the pool and swimming over to the swim-up bar, Susan found reassurance. She was absolutely buoyant in water where her feet could touch.

Then she came to the stool.

She jumped up in her buoyant state to sit down on the seat. Unfortunately, only half a cheek hit the surface.

The rest, dangling mid-water, proved to be too much for the smidgen on the stool. She slid off most ungracefully, nearly dunking herself on the way down.

Her buoyancy had failed.

This, she insisted, occurred while she was surrounded by (again, her words) "a bunch of 20-year-olds in string bikinis."

"Wow," I said sympathetically, once I stopped laughing. "That's embarrassing."

"Nah," she said, the wisdom of her two quarters plus years floating to the surface. "I was 20 once."

(Writer's Note: The subject would like to make it known that her second attempt at the stool was successful, much to her relief, as she hated to have to renounce boating and swim-up bars in the same day.)

What Did the Doctor Say?

As my parents have gotten older, we have found ourselves at the hospital more and more. Mom is the main patient. Dad is the transporter and purveyor of information.

We've known for years that Dad has trouble with the medical lingo. Whenever we ask him a question about what the doctor said, you can see a cloud of confusion glaze across his eyes as he stammers to relay the words of the physician.

"What did the doctor say about Mom's breathing?" we ask.

"Well... ummm..." Dad's brow furrows as he tries to remember. "I think he said it's good...Yes, he said... it's good."

"Good enough to come home?" we pry for details.

"Well, I don't know... He didn't say that..." Dad replies, trying to remember anything he had heard the doctor say.

Turns out, this trait is hereditary. I have it. A couple of my children have it. And, it can be traced to a few extended family members as well. The medical ineptness is so bad, on Mom's most recent trip to the hospital, we determined that all information must be told to my sister, April, and she would tell the family one by one. We can't even have a phone chain. The rest of us cannot be trusted with relaying correct information.

The trip started with Dad taking Mom to the emergency room. On his way back to Mom's bed after going to the restroom, he got lost. He saw a man with his arm around a woman wearing a pink sweater like the one Mom was wearing and asked, "Is that your wife or mine?" The man assured him this pink-sweatered woman was his.

Then I stepped into the picture. Standing by Mom's bedside, rubbing her hand while a nurse took blood, I was watching the monitors above.

"Oh," I said as if I knew something. "She doesn't like that. Look at that bottom line. It was steady and now it's going all crazy."

The nurse, concentrating on the task at hand, ignored me.

I rubbed Mom's hand harder to soothe her. The line went even more haywire.

"Oh my!" I said, with a little edge in my voice this time. "She really doesn't like this! Are you sure everything is OK?"

The nurse looked up and deadpanned, "You're rubbing her finger with the monitor on it. She's fine."

Sure enough, I stopped rubbing Mom's hand and the monitor went back to its normal rise and fall.

I was the only one at the hospital when a doctor came in. He said a bunch of words — something about heart and lungs, and I think capillaries were mentioned. I nodded and thanked him.

My sister arrived later and after looking around said, "I can never find a doctor when I'm here! Where are they?"

"One was just here," I said.

"Which one?" she asked.

"Ummm..."

"Well, what did he say?" she continued, staring me down as if she glared hard enough at me she might be able to read my brain.

Nothing. I could relay nothing.

April took a deep sigh trying her best to be patient, turned on her heels and headed for the nurses' station. I rubbed Mom's hand — the one without the monitor — assuring myself that at least I was good at that.

I was taking my kids to the hospital to see Grandma. I wanted to prepare the youngest one for what he would see.

"She's got some tubes attached to her and there's a lot of machines," I told him.

David responded, "Is she in a concussion?"

He meant "coma," but it didn't really matter. I knew he was destined to have no medical savvy.

A call from my second cousin, Jill, confirmed that my family's medical ineptitude can be traced through four generations. Jill's mom is my mom's aunt.

"I asked my mom what was going on with your mom," Jill said. "She said she had been incubated."

"Intubated," I corrected.

"I know," Jill said with a sigh. "I didn't correct her. There's just no use."

"You're right," I agreed, knowing that it was just a matter of time before my next medical lingo mistake.

Like Brothers

They say it takes a village to raise a child. For my youngest son, David, it just takes one Sloan family.

The Sloans are a family of six who live a block away from us. John and Jen are the parents of four lively sons: Jacob, Cameron, Gavin and Mason. Their oldest, Jacob, is the same age as my youngest of four boys, David.

The first time I met the Sloans, I was standing in their kitchen, talking with Jen. One child was running around us making "zoom, zoom" noises. Two were arguing in the living room, and the faint cry of a baby could be heard coming from a back bedroom.

A strange feeling came over me. I knew this chaos. It was my life 10 years earlier, when my boys were younger, and every minute of the day was filled with activity and trauma.

I think that's why David gravitated to this home. There was a strange familiarity to this family. With his brothers being so much older than him, David missed a lot of the chaos years. Somehow, he found the perfect family to experience it with.

We moved near the Sloans when David was 5. While he would go to play with Jacob, he often ended up playing with his brothers. He reached the status of "Even when Jacob is grounded David is allowed to come over" after a year of family interaction. Now, he knows how to get into their house when they are not home and grab whatever he left there. (He always leaves something there!)

Once, he stayed at the Sloans' for three days and Jacob wasn't even home.

"What did you do?" I asked him.

"Played with the boys," he replied happily.

Mason was the first diaper David ever changed, and it was a dirty one!

The first day that school was out this year, David was up early and headed to the Sloans'.

"I thought you were going to the park with your friends," I said as he was walking out the door.

"No," David replied. "I'm going to go teach Gavin and Mason how to swim."

He calls the Sloans his second family, and we have even given Mrs. Sloan a Mother's Day card.

Every once in a while, David will come home from the Sloans' shaking his head saying, "I just couldn't take the noise anymore."

But it's never long before the quiet gets to him and he heads back to the chaos.

I, too, find myself needing a Sloan family fix every now and again. On those days when I feel like I blinked and my boys were grown, I head over to the Sloans'. Without fail, every time I walk into their house, I get that same, "I've been here before" feeling.

Last year, I took the boys for an adventure to a large municipal park. We saw an old, working mill, a waterfall, weird rocks, a deer, and even a tree with a face on it. Sitting at Steak and Shake after our adventure, I asked them what they liked the best about our trip.

Gavin said, "Da deer." (He has the cutest little lisp!)

Mason liked the tree with the face.

Cameron said he liked the thing hanging from the back of a truck in the parking lot. (It was a disgusting phallic symbol hanging from the hitch.)

They all went into an uproar. "That was awesome!" "Yeah! That's my favorite thing!" "That was the best!" One of them admitted to touching it, which started another round of uproarious laughter and chatting.

I sat back, while all the Steak and Shake patrons stared at us, and basked in the glow of the chaos.

This past Easter, I was feeling a bit sorry for myself. I've always filled plastic eggs for an Easter egg hunt and made clues for the boys to find their Easter baskets.

The older boys had long since stopped hunting for eggs and David was the only one I would be writing clues to find his basket this year.

I was outside, sweeping the patio, thinking about the years past when the boys were younger, when David came trouncing up the drive with all four Sloan boys in tow.

My world immediately brightened.

"David and Jacob," I ordered, "get the plastic eggs out. We're going to have an Easter egg hunt!"

I kept the three younger Sloan brothers busy while David and Jacob filled the eggs and hid them outside. When it was time to hunt, they ran around, excited with every egg they found.

On Easter morning, David's final clue to find his basket led him to the Sloans' house. "Your quest is almost over." The clue read. "Your search is nearly through. Your basket is at the place that is a second home to you."

I was going through David's papers that he brought home at the end of the school year. In a brown bag was a bunch of notes from friends in his class. Apparently, a teacher had made an assignment to write to people in your grade and tell them what you like about them.

I was reading through all the notes, enjoying seventh-graders' interpretations of one another. Some of the notes were long, remembering funny times or crazy things said. Then I came to Jacob's, written on a skinny strip of construction paper. Opening it, I couldn't imagine how he could fit the details of their friendship on such a little piece of paper.

Turns out, he summed it up perfectly in two words. "Like Brothers."

For the Love of Money

My husband, Bill, sent 12-year-old David to the gas station across the street to get change for a $20.

When he told me he had sent David on this errand, I cringed and asked, "Did he know what that meant?"

"Apparently not," Bill replied. David had proudly returned with the change — all $12.67 of it — and two packs of gum and a beef jerky. "I should have just given him the $20!"

He did note that, along with the change, David also gave him one of the packs of gum.

It was a nice gesture, we both decided.

Then, three days later, David was heading out to baseball practice and casually asked, "Hey Bill, are you chewing that gum?"

"Yes, David," Bill replied. "I've been chewing the gum."

David looked slightly disappointed, shrugged his shoulders and headed out the door.

Bill and I looked at each other and started laughing. David's "generosity" had backfired.

The incident reminded Bill of the time he was walking into a store with 10-year-old daughter, Lindsey, and she asked, "What's my budget?"

"Your budget?" he asked, surprised. It seems his generosity of letting her buy a toy or some candy when shopping had turned into an expected expenditure — with a budget!

Lindsey's budget turned out to be zero that day.

I always thought my parents were being ridiculous when they would loudly announce that "Money doesn't grow on trees!" Of course it doesn't. Anyone can see that. I checked them off as absurd and over-exaggerators.

Now, I find myself uttering those very words. Clearly, my children think the green stuff just magically appears in plentiful amounts. And, I am convinced, until bills start showing up in their names, they will not understand the concept of supply and demand when it comes to spending.

My friend, Kathy, was informing her son at college that she found it ridiculous for him to come home to escort his girlfriend to the high school prom.

"That phase of your life is over," she told him. "And besides, it's expensive!"

"Just charge the tuxedo to my account," Anthony impatiently told his mom.

Kathy took a deep breath, trying to control her words and replied, "Anthony, where do you think the money in your account comes from?"

Anthony paused to think about that.

"Me!" Kathy yelled, in disbelief. "If I charge it to your account, I'm still paying for it myself!"

The highly intelligent Anthony opened his mouth to respond, then determined his words might be better saved for a "thank you" later.

18-year-old Trevor received $50 in the mail from his grandmother. His father told him he needed to send her a thank you note.

While holding the $50 bill in his hand, Trevor asked his dad for money to buy a card to send to his grandma. When Dad suggested that Trevor buy the card with the money in the palm of his hand, Trevor explained that he did not want to have a "negative cash flow."

"Well then," Dad replied, with fatherly wisdom. "Don't ever have children."

Feisty, Fun and Fearless — That's my Niece!

Right after my niece, Jamie, was born, my boys were at my sister's house.

When I went to pick them up, 3-year-old Andrew was sitting on the back stoop.

"What are you doing?" I asked him.

"Aunt April has her *own* kid now," Andrew pouted.

Apparently, the boys had been yelled at for being too rough around the baby. This was a new rule for my boys. Aunt April was always fun-loving and crazy. She was like a second mother to them, only better.

The boys came to terms with this new baby. But they weren't quite sure what to do with — a girl.

Their goal became to turn this cute, sweet, bundle of blonde-haired locks into one of them.

Jamie went to kindergarten pounding her chest, saying, "You wanna piece of me?"

The boys taught her the right intonation for "Do you smell what the Rock is cookin'?"

When she came to my house, she would ask to wear the boys' clothes.

When Jamie was 6, I took the boys to her dance concert. They were confused. They had trained her. They had spent hours tirelessly teaching her the ways of power-bombing and chest pumping. Yet, there she was, dressed in a tutu.

The worst part was, they had to admit, she was absolutely adorable dancing to "The Good Ship Lollipop."

The final straw was Jamie's 10th birthday.

We showed up at my sister's house for the birthday party, and Jamie came to the door to greet us dressed in a black and white polka dot dress with a matching headband and purse. Her shoes were a slight heel with bows.

Literally, my boys looked at her in disbelief and said, "Who are you?"

Jamie ignored their stares and welcomed them to her party.

It was official. She was truly a girl. They had failed.

On Jamie's 12th birthday, the boys and a group of their friends decided to exact revenge on Jamie's girliness by toilet papering her house. They made a sign that read, "HONK! Jamie's 12!"

It's been the same every year since. Toilet paper, signage, honking. The only difference is Aunt April requested that no toilet paper be thrown into the gutters of the house. (It clogs.)

Jamie has been the effeminate example of a girl for my house full of testosterone.

When she brought a boy to Easter dinner, my boys just innately hated him. They truly could not come up with one reason why. It's been the same with every boy she has brought around. Not one has a chance.

Two years ago, Jamie arrived at Thanksgiving in a pair of glasses. The boys asked her when she got them and what was wrong with her eyes.

"Oh, I wear these just because I look good in them," Jamie said, adjusting them on her face with style.

There are no words to explain the look on the boys' faces. Confusion and disbelief just don't describe.

That same Thanksgiving, sitting down to the table and passing the feast, Jamie announced that she would not be eating any turkey because she was vegetarian.

"You don't eat meat?" one of my carnivorous boys asked, certain that he had misunderstood.

Jamie, unwavering and quite confident in her response, replied, "As of yesterday, I do not."

For Christmas that year, the boys wrapped up a very large pair of goofy sunglasses and a pound of bacon.

Jamie opened up the crazy sunglasses, looked at her cousins, flipped her long, blonde hair to one side and rolled her eyes.

She opened up the pound of bacon and, totally thrilled, squealed, "Oh! I love bacon!"

One of the boys said, "But you're vegetarian."

Jamie looked at them all and said with the sweetest sarcasm, hugging her pound of bacon, "That was so last week."

She has endured endless harassment about her girly wiles from the boys. When she was younger (right after she started acting like a girl) I think it hurt her feelings. But as she has gotten older, I attribute the boys' hassling to her quick-witted, sharp-thinking nature. She is the queen of one-line comeback zingers.

Through all the rough-housing and badgering, Jamie is adored by her cousins — though they will never fully understand her.

Unbelievably (to me), Jamie just turned 16. Just like with my own children, I feel like I blinked and she is grown.

The day was celebrated with the usual fanfare of toilet paper, signs and honking, with an added highlight of forks stuck in the yard and cotton balls strewn about. (Turning 16 is, after all, a big event!)

We didn't know it, as we were busy tossing toilet paper rolls across tree limbs, but Jamie was home. She snuck outside with a bar of soap and wrote all over the windows of our car.

She had done it once again! The boys were left standing in disbelief as Jamie stood laughing, tossing the bar of soap in her hand.

Feisty, fun and fearless — that's my niece!

Forgot Your Password? Click Here

I believe that when someone is born, along with their name they should receive a given password.

My name has been sufficient for use in any and all legal and non-legal transactions in my life. When my name changed, I had to submit lots of paperwork to the government — and my local pizza shop — that I had, indeed, changed my name.

Changing a name is a big deal!

I need a password like that.

I need a password that sticks with me through thick and thin. One password that works on EVERYTHING in the world that requires a password. One password that, if I decide I want to change it, requires more documentation than my mother's maiden name.

The first password I ever had was for my bank, my PIN code. It is an easy, four-digit number that I can tap into the ATM machine without even looking.

Now, if this four-digit Personal Identification Number is good enough to access all my money in the bank, why can't I use it to buy things on the internet?

Four digits apparently aren't complicated enough for eBay. They need six to twenty characters. (Like anyone can remember 20 characters!) AND it has to be a mix of letters and numbers! They don't let you keep it simple either. The password can't be the same as the user ID. I've tried. They're unforgiving on that rule.

I have forgotten and changed my eBay account password so many times that I don't even try to remember it anymore. I just click "Forgot Your Password?" and click through the steps of resetting it.

It used to infuriate me, having to reset every time I wanted to buy something on eBay, but I have become resigned to the fact that resetting is easier than remembering the password associated to my account. (I am really more of a face-to-face shopper. No store clerk has ever asked me for my password when making a purchase. So there, eBay!)

PayPal nearly put me over the edge with its password rules. It requires eight characters — no more, no less — and a mix of numbers and letters, both upper and lower case!

First of all, I think there should be an asterisk on the eBay site page where you create your eBay password that simply states "PayPal requires eight characters." Then I would have known that my six-character password for buying something on eBay wasn't going to work when I went to pay for it on PayPal!

Requiring two passwords for one transaction is more than my brain can handle. Every purchase should come with a free sample of ginkgo biloba!

I have conquered PayPal, however. Whenever I need to use its service, I choose the "Guest" option. PayPal tells me that my user ID has an account with PayPal. I snub the reminder. Sure, I have to type in all my information, but it's information that I know, information that stays the same, like my ONE given name!

This password frenzy has affected our youth. They have grown up in a password world. They accept a multiple password society, and they perpetuate its complexity.

Several years ago, my son set the password for the wireless router in our house. I gave the child the box with the device in it. I was not quite sure what this router would even do, so I left it to him to set it up and make the magic happen.

And it was magical! Within 20 minutes we were cord-free, sitting inside, outside, anywhere we wanted, surfing the web!

Shortly after this son went off to college, the router took a dive and needed reset. Resetting, of course, required the password.

"It's Arrested Development," Phillip explained over the phone. "With all the 'E's' changed to 3's."

The fact that he chose his favorite television show as a password seemed quirky to me, maybe a little disturbing. Changing all the E's to 3's made my head spin all the way around!

"Who makes a password like this?" My husband asked, ready to throw the router out the window, repeatedly re-typing the password as he forgot to convert an "E."

A friend told me there is an app that remembers all your passwords. This sounded genius to me!

I went right to the App store on my phone to download this brilliant, life-changing technology.

When I typed in my Apple ID password, the screen read: "Your password is incorrect."

Football Moms

There may be no more pathetically funny scene in the whole world than a group of moms watching high school football.

"Why are they kicking a field goal?" my friend Kathy wanted to know on a recent Friday evening, as a group of us sat on the 45-yard line of our home field.

"Because they got a touchdown," Cindy explained.

"I know!" Kathy said, becoming highly agitated. "So why do they get to kick a field goal too?"

"It's for the extra point," Cindy said, waiting for it to sink in.

Kathy burst out laughing. "Oh, right! They're kicking for one point, not three! I don't know what I was thinking!"

We often don't know what we are thinking.

I am certain there are some avid, follow-the-ball, know-all-the-rules kinds of moms sitting in high school stands across America who are hip to what's happening on the football field at every moment. These are not the moms I know.

"Get him!" I yelled very loudly as a player careened down the field.

Barb hit my leg, "We have the ball!"

As I cowered in the stands, Kathy asked, "Who has the ball?"

"WE do," Barb replied.

"I mean WHO?" Kathy said, searching for a program.

"Oh!" Barb said, squinting. "Number. I can't see the number."

"I think it was No. 27," I answered.

Referring to the program, Cindy replied, "We don't have a number 27."

"Well, whoever it was sure had a great run!" I concluded, with an authoritative tone.

"The referee threw one of those flags," Barb noticed.

"He did?" we chimed.

"Now why would there be a flag?"

"Is it against us?"

"The ref is saying we did this," Cindy said, making arms movements like the referee.

"What is that?"

"I don't know."

"Traveling maybe?"

"Well that is just ridiculous!"

A quick check with a fan behind us confirmed that the call was, indeed, against our team for being off-sides.

"I think that was a bad call," I said, and shook my shaker jug in protest. "That makes me mad!"

"Well, that No. 42 is making me mad," Kathy complained. "Do you see how hard he is hitting our boys?"

"He's pretty big," Barb noted.

"There's no reason to hit that hard," Kathy continued.

"That's football," I said, sighing, and launched in to my mantra, "That's why I love golf. Very civil game, hard to get hurt and you can play it forever."

Ignoring my speech because she's heard it a million times, Kathy continued, "They've already hurt one of our players. No. 42 is going to hurt somebody else!" Standing up, she yelled out to the field, "Watch 42!"

"I say after three injuries, the game should be called," I continued to share my gaming philosophies. "If you can't play nice, go home."

"Why are they walking off the field?" Kathy asked, still in a tizzy over 42.

"I think they called a timeout," Cindy answered.

"Well, how many timeouts do they get?" Kathy complained. "An endless number? They've had like five already."

"Maybe there's someone down," Barb suggested.

"Oh no, who is it?"

"I hope it's not one of the boys on our team."

"Maybe it's just a leg cramp."

"That 42 better not have had anything to do with it!"

An annoyed voice from behind us said, "Ladies, it's halftime!"

Perfect Curb Appeal

"I can't wait for summer so I can have a lemonade stand again!" my 9-year-old said excitedly.

His older brothers glared at him and uttered a disgusted, "Hrumph!"

The boys learned valuable lessons about entrepreneurship with last summer's lemonade stand: the importance of location, product pricing and the essence of a company spokesperson.

When the older boys were little, every summer without fail they would set up a lemonade stand by the road.

They would meticulously create a sign using every colored marker they could find. Debates would ensue on how much to charge. Ten cents was not enough, 50 cents was too much. The price was always 25 cents.

Then, dreaming of what they were going to buy with all the money they were going to make, they would sit by the road and wait for customers.

Maybe it was the smell of the cows grazing in the pasture across the road. Maybe it was the cars going by at 45 miles per hour. Maybe it was the fact that there were only about seven cars going by every hour.

There were days when those boys sat out by the road for hours and never served a customer — except themselves.

The greatest sale they ever made wasn't actually a sale at all. They had sat by the road all afternoon and it was approaching dusk. Hearing a car, they hurried to their official business positions. Scrambling across the picnic table to his spot, one of the boys slipped and fell flat on his face. The driver stopped and paid the boys $2 for "a great show."

They tried to give him some lemonade but none was left. They had drunk every drop.

Last summer, when David and his friend Jacob decided to have a lemonade stand, the older boys chuckled to themselves, patted the little guys on the head, and patronizingly said, "Oh, that's a great idea! Good luck with that!"

Living in town now, right on Main Street, the boys had to figure out the best spot for their stand. They chose to put it directly behind the sidewalk, near the driveway.

David and Jacob were in a hurry to get started. Using a black marker, they threw together a sign. They misspelled lemonade, put a dollar sign on it and then crossed it out to make a cents sign and, though the older boys were appalled, charged 75 cents.

When they made their first sale, they came running into the house exclaiming, "He gave us a dollar and told us to keep the change!"

The older boys were unimpressed by the "luck" of the little ones. Two hours and $16 later, they were in shock.

David didn't understand what all the fuss was about. It all seemed pretty simple to him. Make lemonade and sell it. Snap.

Little did he realize, he had the perfect location: hundreds of cars per hour and easy access to his service. He had priced his product with a built-in tip. And, he and his little friend, Jacob, with their messy, misspelled sign, had perfect curb appeal.

About three hours and $24 into their business venture, the boys had enough.

But before we had a chance to dismantle the stand, 13-year-old Andrew and his friend decided they wanted to take a shot at this cash cow.

Forty-five minutes later, the boys came to the realization that their days of lemonade stands had passed. No longer were they "a great show."

"I felt kind of dumb sitting behind that messed up sign," Andrew admitted, recognizing the marketing may not be up to par for his image.

Adding insult to injury, they had two customers, and both wanted change.

Uber and Airbnb

My son was moving into a new apartment, so I was heading to Chicago to assist, looking forward to seeing the new place. I was also going to be meeting his girlfriend's mother for the first time, making the trip even more fun and exciting.

As I went to book a room, I discovered the area he was moving to didn't have any hotels. If I stayed a few miles away, close to his old apartment, I would have to taxi back and forth.

Phillip suggested I try Airbnb.

"Air what?" I asked.

I was informed by the child that people post rooms or entire apartments or homes on this site to rent. Visitors browse the listings, then message a host, requesting to stay.

It sounded a little sketchy to me.

"Everybody does it," Phillip informed me.

Feeling trendy, I tossed my hair back like a twenty-something and went to the site.

As I casually perused the listings, I started to think this might not be such a bad idea.

There was the "Cozy Studio in Uptown," and a "Comfy Room near the Lake" and an "Art Collector's Greystone Apartment."

Pictures of the hosts were at the bottom of every listing. They all looked to be in their 20s and 30s.

"I can do this!" I determined. So, I set out to find a host.

"I am coming to Chicago to help my son move," I emailed potential hosts. "I will also be meeting his girlfriend's mom for the first time!" I went on to explain the days I would be in town and that I would not be much of a bother, as I would be spending most of my time out and about the city.

Apparently, I reeked of middle age. (Phillip said I sounded stuffy.)

Cody and his wife replied, "Thanks for reaching out. Unfortunately, we cannot host you on those days."

Vivian emailed me back, "I'm sorry but those days are not available. I hope you find a nice place to stay."

A sweet, young woman named Mandi took pity on me and agreed to approve my request. However, she cautioned me, "I just want to make sure you know that the bed is an air mattress."

That would be a big no thank you!

I was ready to let my middle-aged fingers do the walking and book a room in a hotel the old fashioned way, by phone. But my trendy side filled with resolve. I was going to do this!

So, I revised my request a bit. Short, sweet and to the point, with a little bribery.

"I am traveling to Chicago to move my son. I will also be meeting his girlfriend's mom for the first time," I wrote, just as before. But then I threw in my ringer. "I am clean, quiet and I come bearing Ohio wine."

They couldn't approve me fast enough!

Jasmine, Lena, Cate all welcomed me with open arms.

I ended up choosing a host named Damian with a "Cozy Room with Skylight." It was the closest to Phil's new place.

I arrived after 11 p.m. the first night. Damian and his brother greeted me, and we shared a glass of wine while we chatted. Damian is an aspiring actor, and his brother is a law school student. Both make ends meet by giving Segway tours.

They were friendly, welcoming, charming young men, and I went to my "cozy room with skylight" that night pleased with my choice to leave my middle-aged comfort zone and try this newfangled Airbnb fad.

That was the last I saw of the brothers. I stayed three nights in my cozy room. I came and went as I pleased. When I packed my bags to leave, I left the key on the kitchen table with a note of thanks.

As I was leaving the city, feeling empowered by my new-found trendiness, I said to Phillip, "I want to try this Uber thing."

"You need to download the app for that," he informed me.

I glared at him over my reader glasses. I was trendy enough for now.

I hailed a cab the old-fashioned way. I raised my arm and yelled, "Taxi!"

Hire Me!

I was driving home from work when I got a phone call from my son.

"Mom!" 14-year-old David said excitedly. "I'm going to get a job at the Dairy Queen!"

"You are?" I said. "How do you know they will hire you?"

David replied, "Because I went in and asked for an application, and they gave me one!"

I laughed. I wish it were that simple. But I wasn't going to rain on his enthusiasm.

"Well good for you!" I said.

The poor kid. He wanted to work at a local farm last summer. I took him to the farm office and instructed him to ask for an application. The woman looked at him and asked him how old he was. When he said he was 13, she said she was sorry.

"Because of new government regulations, I can't hire anyone younger than 16 anymore," she explained. Looking at me, she said, "And I'll never see him when he's sixteen. He won't want to work this hard then." We both knew she was right.

I've gone through this with all my kids at this age: old enough to spend money (and lots of it!) but too young to earn any.

By the time I got home, David had his Dairy Queen application filled out. He was very excited, and I was curious to learn more about the Dairy Queen's hiring young kids. As I read through his application, I realized I would probably not have a chance to find out about their hiring practices as the child was very likely NOT going to get called for an interview.

He filled out his name, address and phone number just fine. The next question was, "Are you available to work weekends?" He answered, "Yes."

"When are you not available to work?" David answered, "Saturday and Friday."

"David!" I yelled. "First you say you can work weekends and then you write not Friday or Saturday!" He said he wanted to have some time to spend with his friends. "Do you want to get hired or not?" I asked impatiently. He erased his two unavailable days.

The next question was, "Are you available to work on holidays?" David replied yes to all holidays except the Fourth of July.

"Why can't you work on July 4th?" I asked.

"Because I have things to do that day," David replied. I didn't bother to ask what "things" he had to do because I was distracted by his essay.

"I have never had a job before. I've always loved DQ. I always go there in the summer." David wrote. "I really would like to work with everyone there. And if possible I'd like my friend Connor to get a job."

"David!" my voice was shrill. "You can't request that they hire your friend!"

"Why?" he asked. "We both want to work there."

Shaking my head, I continued to read.

"I need to get money because I'm tired of asking my mom for some. I'll do any job you ask me to do. Well, I hope you give me a job! I could use the money."

Not a bad ending, I thought. Then I noticed the colon, parentheses at the bottom of his essay — the texting generation's emoticon for a smiley face — right there, at the end of the child's job application.

This is why no one hires 14-year-olds, I thought to myself. But, I smiled at David, gave him an encouraging pat and said, "Turn it in! Hopefully they will call!"

Sitting and Spinning

If AAA had a no-call list, I would be on it.

I am a huge fan of the auto club, celebrating 10 years of membership this year.

They, however, are not a huge fan of me or my car. I believe I will have to change my name and buy a new car to get a membership next year.

It all started with the first big snow of the season. When I picked up my son after school, he had to push me out of the parking lot.

"We need to head home now or we're not going to make it!" I said in a panic as big, fat snowflakes hit the windshield.

I held my breath most of the way home, slipping and sliding the entire way. As we pulled onto our street, I breathed a sigh of relief. "We made it!"

Then the car stopped. The small incline on our road was too much for my trendy, little, winter-hating car. The snow won.

David got out to push once again, but the spinning tires would not move forward.

"Get your stuff," I said. We trekked home.

I called AAA. "This isn't an emergency," I told them. "Please take care of others who are stranded first. I just need my car towed home."

"Where is the car, ma'am?" the AAA operator asked. I gave her the street name.

"Where do you want it towed?" she asked.

I paused before I answered. "About one-tenth of a mile up the street."

I could sense the eye-rolling on the other end of the phone.

When the tow truck arrived, the driver was visibly rolling his eyes.

"I'll make a path ahead of you, just follow my tracks," he said.

"Ok," I answered. "But I don't think it will work."

It didn't.

He hoisted the car and pulled it the 18 seconds it took to get it home. As he backed into the driveway he suggested, "Put the garage door up and I'll slide it inside."

"Oh, that's all right," I protested. "I can get it from here." He dropped the car, pulled away and I sat and spun the wheels two feet from the dry, warm garage. David, once again, provided the nudge I needed to get moving.

That's how I have spent much of this winter, sitting and spinning in one location or another. David has become an expert pusher, and so have a few of his friends.

In hindsight, I probably should have considered the effects that all that sitting and spinning would have on my tires, but I did not.

Until last Friday.

It was 10:30 p.m. with me and three teenage boys in the car on a dark and deserted road, (of course!) when the back, passenger tire blew. While all three boys were well-versed in pushing, a lack of tools made it impossible for them solve this new issue: sitting with no spinning.

It was AAA to the rescue once again. The driver had the spare tire on in short order, and we were on our way.

For 2.8 miles.

"That doesn't sound good," said one of the boys in the back.

I pulled over. The spare was flat. I called AAA.

"Oh my goodness!" the dispatcher exclaimed. "Let me catch him before he gets too far away!"

My trusted AAA savior arrived at our new location and pumped up the spare.

"Can't you just tow it?" I asked, just wanting to get home.

"You're fine!" he said. And off I went down the road.

Another two miles later, the noise was back. I had AAA on the phone before I even pulled over.

"The tire's flat again!" I said, exasperated. I stopped and David got out to look. Just as the dispatcher was hurriedly hanging up to call the driver once again, David yelled from outside the car, "It's not flat!"

"What? It's not flat?" I asked, confused.

The dispatcher repeated what I said, "It's not flat?" Then, with a tone of irritation, "Is the tire flat?"

David confirmed the tire was, indeed, round and full of air.

Sheepishly, I said into the phone, "I guess it's not flat."

Before I could even apologize, she hung up. AAA had enough of me for one day!

The next morning, I went directly to the local tire shop. They were appalled at the condition of my treads.

"The car is rear wheel drive," the tire expert informed me. "You need snow tires."

Problem solved! No more sitting and spinning! He also told me the spare tire was a size bigger than the rest of the tires, thus the loud noise.

I thought about calling AAA and informing them of my findings. But, I decided it might be best if they didn't hear from me for a while.

Doin' the Stick Shift Dance

A few days before my youngest son turned 15 ½, I said to my husband, "I don't think I can do this again."

I found myself having near panic attacks, re-living the horrors of teaching my three older sons to drive — the clutching of my door handle around bends, the stomping of my imaginary foot brake, the pounding of my heart.

If I weren't so tired of hauling this kid around everywhere, I probably would have made him wait until I was old and in a comatose state to let him drive.

Somewhere between David turning 15 ½ and the drive to the BMV (which was precisely the same day), I gained my composure. I reasoned that the other three didn't kill me when they were behind the wheel, so the odds were in my favor that this one wouldn't either. Somehow, this was reassuring to me.

He passed the permit test with flying colors. As all the other times I have left the BMV with a child who has a brand spanking new picture of himself with height, weight, hair color and a state-issued identification number, I tossed him the keys.

I can't decide if I truly am not afraid of my offspring behind the wheel any longer or the kid is actually a really good driver. I didn't clutch, stomp or pound the entire way home.

Perhaps it was the ease at which David learned to drive.

Maybe I'm bored with the whole new-driver scenario and decided to shake it up.

Or, I could just have an evil, sadistic side.

A week after David starting driving, I picked him up from school in my little, white car. "We can't keep driving that big car. It's costing a fortune in gas," I told him. "If you're going to drive, you're going to have to learn to drive a stick shift."

The look of horror on his face subsided just a little as I tapped the driver's seat with a smile and said, "Come on. Get in. You can do this!"

We jolted, jutted, popped, bumped, stalled and re-started our way around the school parking lot as I coached him.

"It's like a dance," I explained, moving my hands back and forth portraying the motion of the gas and clutch pedals.

I repeated this mantra after every stall and start.

"I don't know what that means!" David finally yelled, exasperated.

I fell silent. The "dance" was my only advice. It was my entire stick shift teaching curriculum.

After four or five times, bumping and jolting across the parking lot, he had successfully popped it into first and found second gear.

"Let's head home!" I waved my hand out to the road in dramatic fashion.

David shook his head, took a deep breath and headed toward the street.

Oh sure, we looked like a cow choking on a chicken bone every time he shifted gears, but other than those hiccups, he did fabulous!

Until we came to a stop sign on a hill.

"This is going to be hard," I forewarned him. But the sadistic side of me made him try.

I put the flashers on, opened up the sunroof and waved three cars past us as he sputtered and stalled repeatedly.

Not wanting him to get discouraged, I finally got behind the wheel, negotiated the hill, and then put David back in the driver's seat.

He hopped back in, popped it into first and off we went once again.

I marveled as he drove down the road. I don't think I would have made it out of the school parking lot with one of the other boys without freaking out. And if we had, the stick shift driving days would have been over by the time the flashers went on and the first car went past us on the hill.

Was he a really good driver or was I just calm, cool and collected?

When he pulled into our driveway, a sense of relief flooded over him.

"I can't believe I made it!" he confessed.

"Of course you made it!" I patted him on the back. But to be honest, I couldn't believe it either.

Whose Money Is It?

"Mom, I need to open a bank account," David informed me over the phone, after his first day of work as a lifeguard at the local pool. Questioningly he continued, "They said they put money right in the account? I don't, like, get a paycheck?"

"That's direct deposit," I responded.

"Yeah, yeah, that's what they said it was!" David felt reassured.

"I'll meet you at the bank," I told him.

It was a long haul, but my 16-year-old's search for his first job had finally ended.

The journey started the summer David turned 13 and had discovered that he liked money but didn't seem to ever have enough of it.

"I heard that the farm in town hires kids," he told me.

I took him to apply. The owner looked at him, asked him if he was 16 and when the child shook his head, she looked at me and said, "New government regulations don't allow me to hire anyone under 16 anymore." Looking at David she concluded, "And when he's 16, he won't want to work this hard."

When he decided at 14 that he wanted to work at the local Dairy Queen, which supposedly hired 14-year-olds, he filled out the application requesting that his friend, Connor, be hired too, concluding with, "I hope you hire me. :)" (the millennial's emoticon for a smiley face) I laughed hysterically.

They did not call. He did not understand why.

Now 16, I was adamant about him finding a job this summer. He applied at every restaurant, grocery store and pizza shop.

"Why aren't they calling!" he lamented one evening.

"Are you still using that smiley face thing at the end of your applications?" I asked.

He rolled his eyes, "No mom!"

"There's always the farm," I suggested.

No comment. (The farmer was right.)

He finally got a call from a local restaurant looking for a dishwasher. I found this idea quite amusing, as one shift would involve the child washing more dishes than he has washed in his entire life!

Just as he was settling in to dishwasher mode, the local pool hired him as a lifeguard. He had decided to take a lifesaving course, which I thought was odd, believing he would never get hired at a pool this summer.

I was wrong. He was thrilled.

I was a bit nervous. Dropping a dish as a dishwasher is a completely different level of responsibility than saving a drowning child.

Our trip to the bank didn't help calm my nerves.

"Yeah, I'm a lifeguard," he told the lovely banker wryly as she started working on the paperwork. "Enforcin' rules, savin' lives," he smiled, while I rolled my eyes and the banker chuckled.

After two trips to his car for paperwork he neglected to bring in, he was ready to choose his debit card design. Looking over the choices, he decided on the card with a puppy and kitten on it.

"Well, that's great," the banker told him. "Every time that card is chosen, we make a donation to the Humane Society."

David smiled, feeling good about that and then his face became serious as he asked, "Wait, whose money do you use for that?"

The banker laughed. "Don't worry! We make the donation!"

Next was his user name and password. He chose a nickname his oldest brother gave him when he was little, Dudey, and his favorite number. He had to add "The" in front of Dudey to make it long enough.

I was shaking my head.

When he answered his security questions, the banker and I both had to laugh out loud.

Question 1: "Who is your favorite author?"

David typed in his last name.

"Your favorite author has the same last name?" I asked, surprised.

"No, it's me. I write stuff I like."

Question 2: "Where were you born?"

David typed, "Hospital".

He tried to use his last name again for one of the other answers but the system would not let him, so he added a "y" to the end.

I was speechless by the time he was done. The banker was greatly humored.

"Well, you're done," she said. "Your card will arrive in seven to 10 days."

David got up, said "Thanks!" and slapped her a high-five.

I walked out of the bank fervently praying for TheDudey to have permanent duty at the shallow end of the pool!

World's Okayest Mom

"I have a question to ask you," I said to my 17-year-old son, David, "but I don't want you to get mad."

"No guarantees on that," he responded jokingly.

"What time do we have to be there tomorrow?"

Exasperated, David replied impatiently, "Four o'clock, Mom. I've told you three times."

"I know, I know." I said, putting my hand to my forehead and shaking my head. "I just couldn't remember for sure."

David walked away shaking his head.

He thinks I've lost my mind.

Truthfully, after raising four kids, I think he may be right.

Year after year, one child after the other, my mind has slowly deteriorated to mush.

It started with my inability to finish a sentence.

"I was at the store the other day and I saw ..." I will begin.

Then as if someone yelled "Squirrel!" my mind shuts down and shifts to another thought, or no thought at all.

After waiting patiently for me to finish my sentence, an annoyed child will ask, "Who, Mom? Who did you see?"

"Who did I see?" I'll respond.

"At the store!"

The saddest part is, even after the child prompts me with the details to remember, often, the thought is just gone. No amount of coaxing brings it back. It's lost in the black hole of my mind.

This trait is exacerbated when I attempt to verbalize a mental list.

"Andrew, I need you to cut the grass and ..." I begin.

He waits patiently as he sees my eyes roll upward, straining to remember the second part.

I rarely remember what comes after the "and."

"Yep," he says, disrupting my determination to remember. "I'll go cut the grass. Let me know if you ever remember the second thing," he yells as he walks outside shaking his head.

Remembering No. 2 shouldn't be so hard.

David wishes I could remember No. 4.

The youngest of the four boys, he's getting the tail end of my parenting.

"Glad you're really sticking it out to the end," he says one evening, as he's plopping leftovers onto a plate for the second night in a row. "Glad you're giving it the old one-two try. You've got two more years, Mom. Can you make an effort?"

"Oh, it's not two years," I inform him. "It's a year and a half!"

"Really, Mom?" he feigns disgust. "Have you started the countdown?"

To be honest, I have.

It was three weeks before Mother's Day and Andrew announced that he had bought me a present.

"Well, I don't care what it is," I said to him. "Mother's Day is weeks away, and you not only remembered, you bought me something!"

I was thrilled.

"Do you want to know what it is?" he asked.

"No," I said. "I don't even care what it is. I'm just so impressed that you thought of Mother's Day so far in advance."

"It's a mug," he said, the words practically jumping out of his mouth. (Andrew has never once bought a gift that he hasn't revealed immediately.)

"It says, 'World's Okayest Mom'," he announced, beaming.

He waited for my reaction.

I stared at him.

Then I burst out laughing, "That's hilarious!"

When the mug arrived in the mail a few days later, I was instructed to open the package immediately.

"Really, I can wait until Mother's Day," I told Andrew, but he insisted.

Pouring coffee into my pre-Mother's Day "World's Okayest Mom" mug, I smiled.

World's Okayest Mom — I'm alright with that.

Adventures of Off-Roading

I take great pride in the fact that I have never had an accident in a car on a designated roadway.

Off-road vehicles are another story!

By "off-road vehicle" I mean the lawn tractor "off-roading" in my yard.

"Why, when I lift up the hood of the tractor, does it droop to one side, completely off the hinge?" my husband wanted to know one evening.

My knee-jerk reaction was to blame the kids. My second thought was to blame a tree limb. Would it be too outrageous to blame the dog?

While I was deep in contemplative thought, my husband glared at me, not wanting to hear a tall tale.

Realizing I was busted, I threw my hands up in despair and wailed, "There are so many things to maneuver around!"

The decorative wooden fence had been the culprit in this incident.

The volleyball pole was the reason the rubber flap that helps shoot the grass out directionally no longer shoots anything directionally.

The large landscape rocks were the reason for the scratches, smudges and dings on the once-pristine paint job of the mower.

"Our yard is like an obstacle course!" I pleaded my case.

"No," my husband said firmly. "No, it isn't."

While off-roading on the tractor, I contemplate many things.

Just how many sticks can hide in a yard?

Thousands.

How far can a small stone shoot out from a mower?

Really far.

Did we really need to put this fire pit here?

That's affirmative.

Then, there are occasional moments of wisdom. Rubber balls do not scoot out of the way when nudged by a tractor. They are swiftly sucked into the blades and spit out the other side in millions of colorful shards.

And as much as you try to tell yourself that it looks like a party in the yard, as you look behind you to survey the area, it, indeed, just looks like a damn mess.

By the middle of summer, the lawn tractor was nothing less than a disaster.

The blade was so bent and crooked, half the lawn got a buzz cut and the other half didn't get cut at all. It looked like an angry hacker had attacked the property.

Bill asked, "How did this happen?"

"I don't know," I replied, although I did have a slight recollection of trying to mow over a rut.

Finally, the poor, worn out lawn mower just refused to start. It had had enough.

That's when the hero of all off-roading lawn equipment entered our lives: the zero turn mower.

"Sweet" and "awesome" were just a few words the kids used to describe the new machine.

"You!" Bill said, rudely pointing a finger in my direction, "are NOT allowed on this."

I put my hands on my hips indignantly.

"Really, Mom," Andrew echoed Bill's sentiment. "Don't try to drive this."

I put my hands in the air as in surrender. "Not a problem!"

So, the thing is, last week Bill was out of town and Andrew ended up working late. I checked the weather and it was going to rain for the next five days.

The grass had to be cut now.

I looked at the machine. I sat on it. Just so happened, the key had been left in it. I started it. That was easy!

It didn't seem to want to move. I pulled a lever and the zero turn inched forward. I clutched the handle bars. Whoa! The slightest movement and the machine turned sharply.

I had second thoughts about going any further. This was more off-roading power than I had ever experienced.

I pushed on the bars and moved the mower out the door into the grass. I had reached the point of no return.

It was time to mow.

Unsure of how to engage the mower, I found a red button and pushed it. Immediately, I heard the blades whirling beneath me.

The first few rounds across the yard were rough, but I found my rhythm with the bars and started feeling confident. I was quite proud of myself when I was done!

The next morning, I ushered Andrew to the front door.

"See what I did?" I shared proudly.

After the look of horror left his face when he realized I had been on the zero turn, he studied the lawn and asked, "Did you lower the deck?"

"Yep!" I said, proudly. "I pushed the red button."

"The red button starts the blades, it doesn't lower the deck," Andrew informed me. "You have to push the foot pedal and release the pin and lock it in place."

"You have to do what?" I asked, confused. "But it worked, the grass is cut."

"No," Andrew answered. "You spent an hour and a half lopping off the top of dandelions."

Chaperones Under Fire

I don't know exactly how I got talked into it.

Somehow I ended up on a school bus at midnight, headed an hour and a half away as a chaperone for the after prom.

My friend Kim was my partner-in-chaos. I've known Kim for more than 15 years. We've been long-suffering moms even longer. She, too, wondered how she had ended up on this detail.

"I'm bringing a trivia game to play on the bus," I informed her a week before our overnight trip.

"That will be fun!" she said, both of us desperately trying to be encouraging about this fated night.

"I have a dry erase board," I continued. "We'll play boys against the girls or left side of the bus versus right!"

This made us excited about the hour and a half ride.

"I'm glad you won't be on my bus," David, my son and 17-year-old prom attendee, informed me. "No one wants to do that, mom."

I packed the trivia cards and dry erase board in my car at 11:30 p.m. When I got to the bus, I chickened out and kept them in the car.

I think I will always regret not torturing these kids with a competitive trivia game on the bus on prom night.

Once on the bus, I said to Kim, "This isn't so bad. But when did they make the seats so close together?"

Halfway through the trip to the "funnest place on earth," the bus driver turned the lights on and announced, "No obstructing the aisle. Sit up."

I looked at Kim and whispered, "I think we are supposed to be watching for stuff like that."

She looked concerned and agreed. "Glad he caught that," she said.

Then, we noticed the prom couple in front of us were slouched down in their seat.

"What are they doing?" I mouthed to Kim.

She shrugged.

I tapped the head of the boy.

He turned around to look at me.

"So, Caleb, what are you going to do after high school?" I asked him.

"I'm a junior," he replied.

"I know. I know," I acquiesced. "But you must have some idea of what you want to do."

He told me. I nodded. He turned back around and slouched down in his seat again. I looked at Kim and mouthed, "I don't know what else to ask him!"

Finally, at the "funnest place on earth," we parents were ecstatic. There was EVERYTHING to do here: go-carts, bungie jumping, mini-golf, game room, laser tag, bumper cars, roller skating. You name it!

What did the kids do?

They waited in a line to eat.

"Didn't they just eat at the prom?" one chaperone asked.

"I can't believe they're not running around doing everything!" another commented.

The quote of the night came from a dad who had waited an hour to pick up the food because the restaurant didn't have it prepared on time.

"These kids are pigs!" he said.

After they ate, the hoards dispersed to the various entertainment activities.

After the chaperones cleaned up, we decided we were done being chaperones. We wanted to experience the funnest place on earth.

We started with the go-carts. Then, we moved on to the bumper cars. When we arrived at laser tag, we learned that there was just one session left.

We enlisted every chaperone. It was time to take these kids down!

It was a bad sign when we didn't know how to put the vests on. Really bad when we were unsure of what "base" was.

Even worse when the game started.

"Why does it keep telling me, 'Must go back to base?'" one mom yelled under fire.

Kim was in total dismay, "It won't shoot! My gun won't shoot!"

It was a laser massacre.

68,293 to 18,297

"Well, that was close," I announced to our sweaty chaperone battalion.

"It wasn't close, mom," David, in full battle gear, informed me. "We demolished you."

"Well, we had more fun," I informed him.

Indeed, the after prom chaperones may have had more fun than the kids.

Doin' the School Lunch Countdown

I've run the numbers — admittedly, it's a bit off — but my rough calculations figure that I have packed 8,520 school lunches.

Days absent, snow days, class trips and the occasional "I'll buy today" are not accounted for. The general, roundabout number of brown bags I have sent to school with my children in the course of their primary, secondary and high school years is 8,520.

To be honest, I find the number exceedingly disappointing. I feel like I must have packed upwards of at least a million brown bag lunches!

I am now down to my last five.

At the end of the week, I will have packed my last brown bagged school lunch EVER.

I'm trying to be sad about it. But my giddy smile and bounce in my step, are a fruit drink, peanut butter and jelly sandwich, cut-up apple, Doritos and sweet-treat give away — I am ecstatic over this milestone!

The youngest is graduating, and I am (quite literally) making a spectacle of it. "Doin' the lunch bag countdown" is a daily post on my Facebook page. Moms who know this burden are chiming in.

"You gotta put something crazy in the bag on his last day," one mom suggested.

Another mom responded to her reply, "Like all the stuff you used to find after his clothes went through the wash!"

As I've considered the "grand finale" effect I plan to impose, I've reflected on the years and the 8,520 lunches that have brought me to this moment in time.

Due to writing about family matters for 16 years (when my current graduate was in preschool), some of the school lunch saga has been chronicled in newsprint.

Circa April 25, 2003, titled "If I took stock in lunch trades, would I go broke?" regales the food-brokering that went on with my middle schoolers.

"It seems, if you are willing to fork over your precious sugar-laden sweets, you can have just about anything in anyone else's lunch," I wrote, 14 years ago.

"If I have Oreos, I can get anything I want," I quoted Phillip as saying, "with a sly, confident look."

The oldest, Robert, "nodded his head in agreement."

Later that year, I wrote, "It's official: My mind has turned into jelly." Oct. 15, 2003.

"I made a jelly and jelly sandwich this morning. The peanut butter was sitting on the counter right next to the bread." I never used it. I go on to claim that the jelly and jelly sandwich was proof that, "I have completely lost my mind." (The real story-behind-the-story was that I forgot that a friend had asked me to take her child home and I left him at the football field.) The jelly and jelly sandwich was simply proof to the kids that I had lost my mind.

Then, the following year, there was the "Who wins when it's Maker of the Universe vs. Maker of the Lunches?"

The boys wanted to go to a different church and sat, arm in arm, in a doorway refusing to go to Sunday service.

"I was not happy about this. In fact, I was mad as… well, suffice it to say, I was boiling," I wrote.

"As we [my husband and I] were walking out the door, I could not resist one last jab: 'If you don't have time for the Maker of the Universe,' I informed them, 'I don't have time for you.'"

That story details my not making Sunday dinner or getting the boys up for school Monday morning or packing their lunches.

After one day, they all came pleading, asking me to make dinner, pack lunches, help with homework.

"But 'the Maker' had one lesson left. This one was for me." I wrote all those years ago. "Truly, there is a consequence for every action.

Printed in the USA
CPSIA information can be obtained
at www.ICGtesting.com
JSHW062134030224
56271JS00006B/35/J

9 781638 670162

When I dropped David off at preschool the next day, the teacher pulled me aside."

"'We gave David a hamburger for lunch yesterday,' she informed me in a hushed tone. 'He had only an apple and six pieces of candy in his lunch.'"

As that preschooler heads to his last school lunch, I couldn't help but bring back the past. His special last lunch is an apple and six pieces of candy (with a pizza being delivered to the school).

It was simply the best homage to be paid to 8,520 packed school lunches.